Towards Beloved Community

To Dawn,

Best wishes

Towards Beloved Community

*Finding Hope for Religion & Spirituality
in Postmodernity*

Cathal Courtney

Exposure Publishing
England

British Library Cataloguing In Publication Data
A Record of this Publication is available
from the British Library

ISBN 978 1 84685 661 7

First Published 2007 by
Exposure Publishing,
an imprint of
Diggory Press Ltd
Three Rivers, Minions, Liskeard, Cornwall, PL14 5LE,
UK
and of Diggory Press, Inc.,
Goodyear, Arizona, USA
WWW.DIGGORYPRESS.COM

To Phoebe

Acknowledgements

I wish to thank the organisers of the Hucklow Summer School for inviting me to speak at their 2005 gathering. I am grateful to them and to the various people who encouraged me to prepare the papers for publication. Without their goading this book would not have arisen. In particular I want to thank Jean Mason and Shelia Jones for their friendship, kindness and support.

My ideas have taken shape in the context of ministry in Wakefield, London, Glasgow and Aberdeen, and as a member of the Dublin Unitarian Church. I thank all the members and friends of these communities for their support and patience.

My own minister, Bill Darlison, is a good counsellor and able, through his natural modesty and diplomacy, to ground my sometimes incomprehensible flights of erudition. I thank him and his wife, Morag, who, as well as being a friend, is a reminder that altruism and kindness form part of every decent life and every worthwhile idea.

Nick and Sue Webb, great travel companions, hosts and friends, are inspiring people who have, unconsciously on their part, led me to question many of the assumptions on which religion is based. I thank them for their friendship and for the stimulation they so naturally arouse.

Mark Wilson and Sam Taylor – and their very large circle of friends – embody in their lives the qualities of hospitality, kindness and fun. Their friendship is central to my life, and has been pivotal in developing the concepts in this book.

My friend, Guy Bentham, was kind enough to read the manuscript and suggest amendments. We all become more comfortable with what is occasionally an uncomfortable life when others encourage us and affirm our attempts to do something. Along with Frank, Guy has been such a voice in my life and I thank them both. Any errors in the manuscript are, however, down to me.

Oscar the dog withstood the profanities induced by my frustration as a writer. He remained loyally at my feet throughout and knew exactly when to tug on my shoe for a game of catch. Another dog, now departed, Boffin, was a lovely animal and Biddy and Peg who cared for her are among my closest friends. Their open hearts and minds have exerted a huge influence on me and hence on the content of this book.

I wish to thank Louis, Rita, Clare, Siobhan, Mark and Dan for being my family, in whose midst I have found the ground on which to search for meaning and peace in my life. Most of all I thank Dan for being my companion and best friend. He knows the limitations from which this book emerged and his love is constant.

My greatest thanks go to that mysterious presence at the heart of my life, that links me to my fellows and to the world in which I live. No words can ever describe this force, least of all 'god', but I wish to live my life as a response to what I believe is its endless love for us all.

Prologue

Come, said my soul,
Such verses for my body let us write, (for
we are one,)
That should I after death, invisibly return,
Or, long, long hence, in other spheres,
There to some group of mates the chants
resuming,
(Tallying Earth's soil, trees, winds,
tumultuous waves,)
Ever with pleas'd smile I may keep on
Ever and ever yet the verses owing – as,
first, I here and now
Singing for Soul and Body, set to them my
name,

Walt Whitman

Introduction

POSTMODERNISM is one of those terms that fires the passions of people concerned with the content of our culture. Does it exist, or is it just a clever invention of those not gainfully employed? This question has been hotly debated in universities and public houses for some time. On one side are those who claim we are still very much within the parameters of the project called modernity. On the other are those who insist that our ways of understanding and relating to the world have undergone such changes in the twentieth century that a new term is required to describe the shift. The problem is compounded by those who insist on describing certain philosophies as postmodern when the authors of those same philosophies refuse to be categorised in this way.[1] Perhaps the best way to approach the question of postmodernity is to recall what we mean by its alleged predecessor, modernity.

The project of modernity began with the Enlightenment of the eighteenth century, when thinkers began to value reason as the fundamental tool for interpreting the world. Gradually the more ancient systems of interpretation, such as divine revelation, gave way to the logical consistencies of rational thought. When the ancient texts which had supported earlier models of thought were subjected to historical and literary criticism, their assumptions began to crumble and a new age dawned, an age free from the superstitions of the past. As the revolutionaries of late eighteenth century France enthroned a statue of the 'goddess' Reason in Notre Dame it seemed the world as it had been known for almost two thousand years had all but disappeared.

Modernity continued on the path of trusting reason to solve the many problems which faced the human race. Industry moved from the kitchen to the factory, and large numbers of peasants moved from the countryside to the town to make a living from the opportunities this offered. Great advances were made in science and engineering as the power of the Church to curtail and censor human activity continued to wane. Governance itself came under scrutiny as royal houses fell to the demands of democracy. France and America developed new systems of governance, for the people, by the people. Reason was certainly changing things, but was it making things better?

There is no doubt that squalor and abject poverty existed within the world of modernity, but modernity had an answer. Everything, from our knowledge of the natural world to the plight of the factory worker, had to be understood as points upon the path of progress. History, for modernity, was something that continually moved forward. Things may not be perfect now, but reason would ensure improvements. Onwards and upwards forever was the battle cry.

Reason, of course, was not the invention of modernity. Even before the ancient Aristotle had declared human beings to be rational animals, reason was a feature of the earliest societies. Modernity's uniqueness lay in the level of support it gave to the rational faculty. Modernity assumed first of all that there was such a thing as truth and that this truth was compatible with reason. This was its 'meta narrative' – this was the over arching discourse it maintained. In such a world humankind did not need to rely on the ancient scriptures for the truth. Truth could be arrived at by way of natural philosophy.

Modernity created a number of problems for itself. Important among these were the problems brought about by the explosion of industry and commerce. The factory allowed levels of production unimaginable to earlier generations. Such levels of production led not only to the development of the market economy we know today, but also to a lust for further markets and resources. The story of the factory is closely linked to the story of colonisation as European powers scrambled abroad in search of greater wealth.

Such a scramble inevitably led to conflict. It is possible, maybe even necessary, to see the wars with Napoleon in this context. The Congress of Vienna, in 1815, brought about a temporary cessation, but the European powers were never slow to exploit the weaknesses of their neighbours. Napoleon was long dead when the internal problems with the Ottoman and later the Austro Hungarian empires ignited the greed of neighbouring powers and led to further conflict. These conflicts would play a central role in the two world wars where millions of men, women and children were to lose their lives.

When postmodernists speak of the end of modernity they refer to the end of the rational project. They argue that the loss of life in the twentieth century has made people suspicious of the meta narratives upheld by modernity. What was assumed to be the path of progress by modernists has turned out to be a path of despair, desolation and death. Not only do postmodernists reject the assumptions of modernity, many of them reject the possibility of meta narratives at all. In this sense the postmodern world is a subjective world, a world where each of us must carry the burden of deciding for ourselves what has worth and what has not.

Artistically, postmodernism is exp ressed in patterns that often seek to undermine earlier forms. The distinction between high and low art disappears and we are left with a world of subjective expression. It could, of course, be argued that such trends were evident in the modernist period. Perhaps in the area of art our historical paradigm fails.

Literature, which in terms of classification certainly defies the historical development we are dealing with – modernism in literature refers to twentieth century innovations – is also affected by postmodernism as more shelf space is devoted to the babblings of celebrities 'expressing' themselves through their ghost writers, who are often people with much more to say, and better ways of saying it, than the celebrity concerned.

From my perspective (that, it could be argued, is a very postmodern way to start a paragraph) there are enough major shifts in cultural expression to warrant the use of the term postmodern. The arrival and subsequent explosion of youth culture in the twentieth century, the digital revolution, the emergence of globalisation as both a commercial enterprise and as an ingredient of contemporary consciousness, and our failure to find a common vision in the face of such globalisation, are all reasons to make me think that postmodernism is a useful term to help us understand the changes that are taking place around us. When the term is used in this book it is used for its descriptive qualities and, as will become apparent, not as a vision of where I think we should necessarily be going.

In the postmodern world, religion is in crisis. Rejected by the vast majority of people in Western Europe, it nevertheless continues to contain a potency that feeds wars. Having failed in many instances to support its claims in the age of reason, it lingers on the edges of society offering unreasonable interpretations of the world to those too tired to think. It has become a choice for the jaded in a world filled with an almost endless amount of choice.

Occupying an even smaller space on the edge of society are those liberal churches which did not shy away from the demands of reason, but who sought bravely to embrace reason as an aid to the search for God. Perhaps the collapse of reason as a meta narrative has had an even greater effect on them. Willing to go beyond the limitations of doctrine, tradition and creed, they face a world that is just not interested anymore, a population that shows signs of being in touch with the subjective experience of the spiritual, but unable to see how this might be lived more deeply in the context of a religious community. To the vast majority of people religion belongs in the past. It is a meta narrative whose time has long since past.

As a minister at work within the liberal tradition I found myself feeling frustrated and then anxious about the future of my own denomination. The anxiety became more pronounced as I observed the developing vulnerability of many of our churches. The frustration grew as I recognised our continual failure to engage with the world beyond. The frustration and the anxiety made my job almost unbearable.

Then a strange thing happened. I agreed to serve a tiny congregation of five souls in North London. In moving there, expectations were not high, because despite many great ministers in the past, men and women of great integrity, insight and compassion, the congregation had not grown since the first world war. It was, by many, seen to be on its last legs. A dignified end was all that could be hoped for.

The five women who kept that church afloat taught me some important lessons. Chief among these was the importance of celebrating what we already have and not to lament what might be missing. Faced time and again by problems that might make many people turn the lights off and go home, we decided to abandon the burden of worry and embrace instead, as wholeheartedly as we could, the adventure of faith. Central to this adventure was the obligation to keep our door open for other travellers who might come our way.

Understanding the central calling of community to be about love and not self preservation, we examined the ways in which people might feel excluded or unloved if they were to join us. Knowing that it is impossible to carve a future from a gravestone, we explored the ways in which the habits from the past made us unattractive in the present. If we were to follow the liberal tradition's invitation to take responsibility for our own search while loving other people, then that invitation dictated that there be no sacred cows, only a willingness to co create as open a community as possible. Such a decision was not a denial of the past. We understood well the integrity of the tradition we had inherited, but we also understood the need for the inheritance to evolve ways of being in the world today.

Soon the money was found to erect a sign outside declaring us to be a community of seekers, committed to creating and maintaining a community free from sexism, racism, ageism and homophobia. We were not a church with a message to sell. We were a community of seekers with love to share. We admitted our ignorance, but asserted our hope that together our searches can mean more than those undertaken in private. We were also conscious of ourselves as a community of imperfect people and what to do with our imperfections puzzled us on many occasions. We found that when our hearts were in the right place, imperfections could be accommodated and lived with. In fact we learnt that our imperfections, with a little imagination, could be seen as gifts capable of transforming lives. It became a place of forgiveness because we accepted our own needs to be forgiven.

Four and a half years later I left that congregation. When I left it numbered nearly fifty souls and was among the most vibrant and innovative in the denomination. It continues to grow and thrive. There had been no advertising budget, no marketing, and no easy answers to assuage collective ignorance. What was there then?

There was simply a community. Communities exist to support visions and not to support themselves. Communities that support their visions grow. It's as easy as that. If you're reading this book and worrying about the ever declining numbers in your church, then my only advice is to attend to your vision, and not to your survival. The success of a vision cannot be gauged by the numbers supporting it. Nor can its failure be measured by the numbers rejecting it. Visions can only be assessed in terms of the quality of love generated in their promotion.

I have been held in the love of Unitarian and Liberal Christian communities for ten years now. A vision of the liberal religious community will, I hope, emerge in the pages of this book. It is something which has touched me deeply over the last ten years as I have seen it lived through the lives of the many loveable men and women who make up the Unitarian and Liberal Christian movement today. Visions, no matter how fragile or vulnerable, awaken hope and optimism.

This book is an invitation to let go of the worry and attend instead to the vision of the liberal religious community. If we can do this, we will be doing the world a great favour, for, as we shall see, anxiety has become a major problem in today's world. It cries out for an antidote at every opportunity. Are we brave enough to listen to the cry?

Chapter One

Welcome to Postmodernity

ON THE morning of 8 April 1994, Gary Smith came across a gruesome sight when he arrived at a house in Lake Washington to install security lighting. There, dead on the floor of the first floor annex was 27 year old singer, Kurt Cobain. A single gunshot wound, barely visible, gave the authorities all the evidence they needed to conclude that the cultural icon of 'Generation X' had committed suicide.[2]

For many, particularly those on the religious right, Cobain's death was the inevitable outcome of a life spent flirting with the nihilism they so staunchly rejected. On the extreme right some even welcomed the death, seeing it as heralding the end of what they thought was Cobain's harmful influence on the minds of their young.

For his fans the death was a tragedy. They had lost not a messiah pointing the way to a promised land, but a prophet who told it how it was, an artist who, far from promoting anarchy and nihilism, actually drew attention to the rot in late twentieth century society that engendered the nihilism in the first place. For the fans, Cobain was a victim. In the words of Nat Fisher from HBO's *Six Feet Under*, 'he was just too pure for this world.'[3]

In this way Cobain joins the ranks of other icons, such as Vincent Van Gogh, who have brought about their deaths because of a failure to find a sense of home in the world – Cobain even looked like Van Gogh. The suicide note left behind has all the hallmarks of someone who, while frantically trying to fit in, just could not manage to do so. In that note Cobain wrote that he could not 'get out the frustration, the guilt and the sympathy,' he had for everybody. At the same time he acknowledged that he had become a 'self destructive deathrocker' [sic], who, since the age of seven, had become 'hateful towards all humans in general.'[4]

What kind of society provides the context for such a life? What dynamics are at play in a community where a twenty seven year old successful musician opts for a heroin fuelled existence and, ultimately, death? What values lead a young man to experience sympathy for the human race while feeling hatred for it at the same time? These questions inevitably lead us to question the very nature of the society we live in and the culture that arises from it.

It is easy to dismiss someone like Cobain as a tragic victim of youth culture. After all, since youth culture emerged in the mid twentieth century, older generations have tended to perceive it as nothing more than a temporary aberration before sanity is restored with marriage, family and gainful employment. However, more and more anecdotal evidence emerges suggesting that powerful feelings of alienation are experienced throughout the age spectrum. What were once dismissed as the stupidities of youth – feeling misunderstood, isolated and different – are commonly lingering into middle and old age. Frequently surrounded by material comfort, at least in relation to earlier generations and in relation to the poverty on other parts of the globe, the human subject in the Western World is just not happy. We appear imprisoned and yearning for freedom.

Cathal Courtney

When, in 1791, Jeremy Bentham presented the world with his ideal form of prison, the Panopticon,[5] he was most likely unaware that his imaginative proposal would one day have merit as a depiction of human society more generally. Circular in shape, with a central watchtower that could facilitate the close observation of every inmate, the Panopticon marked a shift in the nature of punishment from torture to observation. Bentham himself remarked that he had imagined a system that could survive even the absence of a governor. Once the central structures were in place, the rest could look after itself with little human intervention.

When Michel Foucault examined the history of punishment[6] he was struck by just how prevalent the Panopticon had become, not just in the area of criminal correction, but in society as a whole.[7] Power, which for the older Foucault was always a two way relationship in which the discourse of the powerful established the field of action for everyone, exerts its influence from the central tower. The powerful reside there to serve a number of principles – the content of the discourse – which they claim to be true. The inmates don't need to be taken out and beaten so as to effect compliance. The very possibility that they are being observed is enough to make them conform to the demands of the discourse.

In 1791, Bentham's discourse was played out through a rigorous timetable for the prisoners. Worship, work, instructional reading and short periods of recreation marked each passing day before the inmates were returned to the solitude of the cell each night. Interestingly, worship could 'last no longer than half an hour', presumably because God knew how to work within a timetable. There was no reason to deviate from the formula as set out. Deviance, in fact, could seriously undermine the entire enterprise.

Anyone who reads Bentham's proposals will be struck by their similarities to Orwell's *1984*. Bentham describes a micro society where everybody knows that they may be the focus of observation at any moment. The advance of technology allowed Orwell to imagine new ways in which the Panopticon asserted its presence in society more generally. He paints for us a worrying picture of isolation is a society that has the means to foster human community, but chooses not to. It chooses not to because the discourse it promotes relies on the image of the solitary figure to further its own ends.

There will always be those who see the correlation between the Panopticon and contemporary society as the stuff of conspiracy theories and nothing else. However, it can be difficult to ignore some of the similarities. Unlike say medieval society, where power was held in a complex network from King to squire, today's society is characterised by a concentration of power in certain institutions. Foucault noted the ways in which people acquire power in these institutions. Because knowledge exists within the frameworks of particular discourses, the person who brings expert knowledge to the discourse is awarded with power. Their expertise is seen as authoritative precisely because it upholds the discourse. In this way we are creating a world for the specialist when the complex constitution of the human being and the problems it faces would suggest we are more at home in the world as generalists.

While we can look at these institutions – government, corporations and the like –

we cannot look into them unless we have specialist knowledge at least equal to that of the other experts. Just like the prisoners who could see the watchtower, but who did not see the people inside, today's citizen sees the fortress of power, but is not certain what principles are at play behind its wall. Perhaps more importantly, today's citizen, just like Bentam's prisoner, fulfils the duty of work, if they are lucky enough to have some, before returning to their cell where the inherent loneliness of human nature is compounded by the further loneliness of an efficient world.

Efficiency compounded loneliness in the industrial age by seeing the human subject as a cog in the wheel of industry and not as an inter connected part of a broader interdependent universe. Human creativity, skill and talent were subjugated in the name of planning, procedure and profit. Dickens' *Hard Times* gave us a saddening depiction of this. Where the worker is still required, we see the rational hunger for order still at play: call centres where staff are allowed to show no signs of their individual identity and where the greatest sin is deviation from the script; the banning of headscarves, crosses and other items of jewellery in the name of uniformity, or what some call, ironically enough, 'social cohension.' It's no wonder that countless numbers of people feel unhappy in their work and long for creative utopias that respect the complexity of their natures. The problem for most is that they cannot afford to follow those dreams, given that children have to be reared, bills need to be paid and hungry stomachs need to be fed.

The growing tendency of post modernity to send the worker home adds to the worry. The technologies of postmodernity in many cases do not require workers. Workers can go and be isolated somewhere else. While some argue that being sent home provides an opportunity to be creative, they do not explain how the basic condition required for creativity, i.e. life itself, can be sustained in a capitalist economy without income. The man and woman, who in the past took some comfort just from knowing they were providing for other people, today face a workplace that can disappear as easily as it came, owing to the whims of global capital. Destined to watch their like live out their basest natures on reality TV, they would be forgiven for wanting to get into that central tower to see what is going on. They cannot, however, because they are not experts.

Anyone exposed to socio economic diversity can see the ways in which all of us, rich and poor, suffer from the observable, efficient world of late capitalism. Fundamentally opposed as it is to anything that threatens its efficiency, our capitalist society appears inevitably drawn to sacrifice the multifarious aspects of human nature that do not support its utilitarian ends. Language itself is under attack. While Orwell's nightmare of what language might become is too depressing for many of us to contemplate, we have to at least engage with the ways language is continually undermined by those whose only interest is making a quick buck. In the fast paced global economy many wonder whether there are values other than those that support the market. They wonder whether there is more to life. However, the capitalist society has trained them for the machine. The language which celebrates the non utilitarian aspects of our existence is pointless in a world that only values the functional and our proverbial wonderer is left without a language with which to really wonder. Science Fiction becomes the only rebellious genre and even that is finally limited in scope by the limited language of materialism. Our ability to express the mysterious becomes weaker and weaker. We end up surrounded by plasma screen televisions telling us nothing. The language which helps us engage with the infinite depth of our lives disappears, and we are left with the ranting and rage of Celebrity Big Brother.

There is little space in the panoptical world for depth and mystery. Valuing, as it does, form and organisation, the panoptical world sees 'otherness' as threatening to its overall welfare. Postmodern theorists sometimes refer to this 'otherness' as 'noise'[8] which may go some way towards explaining the popularisation of psychotherapy in today's society. Every morning, noon and night, growing numbers of men and women who keep the corporate and governmental ship afloat make their way into their therapists' suites to express how difficult it all is and how unbearable the 'noise' is to their ears. The pressures of being observed in a panoptical society inevitably result in the anxiety that those 'private' aspects of personality need to be brought under control. The parts of us which do not serve the machine become parts we do not wish to own. Paradoxically, this anxiety of being observed is matched by the anxiety of not being observed. In a world where observation is central, we have learnt to value ourselves by the quality of footage we give to the observers while simultaneously fearing the intrusion this creates. Just who can resist anxiety in such a world? Just who would not want to suppress it all?

That which cannot be suppressed frequently takes the form of sexual, narcotic or violent urges. In the face of such urges the subject can be terrified that their wife, husband, lover, neighbour, employer or friend might discover their secret. It's saying something that these people turn to a paid stranger for help. It's enough to make me think that we have reached a point where society's pressures are just too much to live with. As Seàn O'Casey observed while putting the finishing touches to *In The Shadow Of A Gunman*, the human being has enough problems to deal with by virtue of their inherent humanity, without society adding to the burden.[9]

The self help gurus have emerged in response to the pain. Firstly, their very title is interesting: SELF HELP. In a world where our understanding of self seems to be part of the problem, these gurus appear to have bypassed the problem entirely. They can help me lose weight, change my aura, win friends and influence people. They can assist me in finding my life's work, improving my pulling power and increasing my productivity, all in ten easy steps. And to top it all, the answer to everything is this thing they call SELF. My failures, my ugliness, my fat, my bad aura, my lack of friends, my wonky chakras, my low productivity are all down to ME. 'Take charge of Your Own Life' – the mantra of self help. It seems that while expert at generating alienation, the panoptical society is reticent about taking responsibility for the alienation it generates.

In a world designed for only a fraction of our human nature, the commercial bit, it is nothing short of cruel to suggest we can overcome the anxiety of our loneliness by becoming better acquainted with the insulated egos the Panopticon exploits. While loneliness may be an anthropological constituent of every person, the ways in which this loneliness is compounded in the Panopticon need to be addressed. We need to recognise the limitations of the discourse we maintain. We need to recognise that the cold, callous world of the panoptical discourse is damaging to all of us. And it is not enough to recognise it; another discourse needs to be put in place, one that is more generous to the complex web of human nature.

Allowing for even a fraction of such an analysis of contemporary society to be true makes it possible to understand the strength of the alienation felt by Kurt Cobain and his 'Generation X'. It certainly helps us to understand why, while enjoying levels of material comfort unimagined by earlier generations, today's population is ridden by alienation and angst. If religion hopes to play a worthwhile role in creating a better society, it must evaluate its own role in supporting the discourse that is ultimately damaging to the human subject. It must discern what is Caesar's and shoulder the yoke of what is not. It must be brave enough to acknowledge the ways in which it has fed the alienation, and creative enough to imagine new discourses which liberate, rather than enslave.

Chapter Two

Religion and Spirituality
in Postmodernity

I leant upon a coppice gate
When Frost was spectre grey,
And Winter's dregs made desolate
The weakening eye of day.
The tangled bine stems scored the sky
Like strings of broken lyres,
And all mankind that haunted nigh
Had sought their household fires.

The land's sharp features seemed to be
The Century's corpse outleant,
His crypt the cloudy canopy,
The wind his death lament.
The ancient pulse of germ and birth
Was shrunken hard and dry,
And every spirit upon earth
Seemed fervourless as I.

At once a voice arose among
The bleak twigs overhead

In a full hearted evensong
Of joy illimited;
An aged thrush, frail, gaunt, and small,
In blast beruffled plume,
Had chosen thus to fling his soul
Upon the growing gloom.

So little cause for carolings
Of such ecstatic sound
Was written on terrestrial things
Afar or nigh around,
That I could think there trembled through
His happy good night air
Some blessed Hope, whereof he knew
And I was unaware.

Thomas Hardy, *The Darkling Thrush*

It was the pop singer Madonna's
wholehearted support of Peter Berg's
Kabbalah Institute that prompted *Guardian*
columnist, Sarfraz Manzoor, to coin the
term 'decaffeinated religion.'[10] Manzoor
legitimately questioned Berg's reduction of
Jewish mysticism to a series of twenty
second speed meditations and his
contention that the ancient Kabbalah texts
no longer needed to be read, only touched.
Moreover, Manzoor drew attention to

the ways in which groups such as Berg's allowed the efforts of personal discernment to make way for the advice of the guru.

Berg, of course, is not alone in allegedly offering quick and easy answers for a set price. The fact is every year sees more and more additions to the list of what some call neo religious movements. Ironically, as traditional religious communities decline more of these new organisations emerge. Their obsession with individual enlightenment, individual development and individual health can stand in insulting juxtaposition to the pain and suffering in the world. While expert at locating the spiritual impulse within the individual, they frequently deny the ancient wisdom that our individuality means little if it is not connected to a sense of our commonality.

A recent study, undertaken by scholars at Lancaster University, chose the town of Kendal, Cumbria (population 28,000) to examine contemporary trends in religious and spiritual practice in Britain.[11] The study concludes that in 30 years time Christianity will be overshadowed by what they term 'spirituality.' Using the example of a recently founded meditation centre in the village of Dent, just outside Kendal, they highlight how people are drawn to a place 'not affiliated to any religion and [where] there is no belief system imposed on anyone.'

The book is compelling reading for those interested in the future of religion and it raises one of the questions I am posing here: why is 'religion' rejected and 'spirituality' embraced?

James Joyce once wrote that, 'there is no heresy or no philosophy which is so abhorrent to the church as a human being,'[12] and he was right. People have rejected religion because, with a few noble exceptions, religion has rejected people. Somewhere along the line, European religion embarked on a course of abstraction which has left it utterly meaningless for the vast majority of people who wish to use their brains. It is, perhaps, helpful to understand this departure in terms of corporate neurosis because it constitutes a fundamental departure from the core identity of religious bodies: to promote loving and just relationships in response to the individual's experience of mystery.

We had a good example of the neurosis afflicting religion today when some months ago the Anglican bishops of the world gathered in Armagh, Northern Ireland to denounce the consecration of a gay bishop in New Hampshire, USA. What added poignancy to the occasion was the plight of the people of Darfur whom the bishops choose to ignore that weekend, opting instead to remain focused on the gay question. Many felt their humanity violated, not only because of the Anglican dismissal of homosexuals, but because the bishops placed such a dismissal as a priority before the terrifying experience of a people facing genocide. Moreover, an institution which claims to care in response to Christ's care for us, found it acceptable to harass and demean the sexual identity of one tenth of the world's population.

'What planet are they on?' – the response of one friend – seemed to sum up the entire experience. Their actions, of course, constitute only one example of western religions' failure to engage with the broad swath of compassionate, intelligent people in our society. The source of this problem lies in the singular fact that metaphysical speculation, married to the neurosis of sexual repression, takes precedent over the infinite value of the human subject. Clerical and academic elites allow their often sex starved, body hating speculation to exist independently of the human experiences that give rise to the speculations in the first place. Traditionally this approach has led to witch hunts, heresy trials and pogroms. The great battlegrounds of metaphysical speculation in the Christian Church – monotheism, Christ's divinity, sources of religious authority – are, thankfully, no longer battlefields, at least for the secular mass. They are merely manifestations of the great decaffeinated religion which has nothing meaningful to say to the vast majority of people on the planet. If the problem of neo religious movements is that they place an unhealthy emphasis on the individual, then perhaps the failings of their more traditional counterparts is that they do not place enough. The human person becomes reduced in value, and, ultimately, serves as nothing more than a means to a speculative theological end.

In a further twist of irony, the alienation examined in the previous chapter would appear to yearn for interpretations of the world that transcend the merely materialistic. Religions, as the harbingers of non materialism, would appear well placed to engage with the alienation. However, they are failing to do so, and this failure is largely linked to religions' refusal to get down in the dirt where they belong and offer truthful descriptions of the human predicament. The fact is that all of us face truly enormous questions in our lives. We have occasions when we think, is this it? Is life simply about paying bills, growing old while working too hard and then dying? And what about the world in which we live and into which our children are born? How can the violence and hatred in that world be brought to an end? Religion is done a great disservice when it concerns itself predominantly with sexual ethics, respectable clothing, good manners, polite social intercourse, cake bakes and tombolas.

Liberal religionists may object, citing their long held inclusive and non judgemental ethos. So, why are people also rejecting these liberal religious communities? There are those who argue, with some justification, that the public perceive us to be just another church, sharing the same neurosis as the rest. After all, the thinking goes, we look like a church, we call ourselves a church, so we are, in fact, a church. From this point of view, the issue facing liberal communities is one of branding. We need to be out there selling ourselves as something fundamentally different in nature from those churches offended by the human person.

There is no doubt that the liberal lamp needs to be taken from beneath the proverbial bushel and allowed to shine. However, just what is it we seek to illumine the world to? Every sect is sacred? Paddle your own canoe? Believe whatever you want to believe, whatever its effects?

The fear of its own demise has caused a neurosis in the heart of liberal religion also. It is the neurosis of individualism. Confronted by the self centredness of the postmodern age, liberal religious organisations repudiate anything that might compromise our highly valued and hard won individualism. Loyalty to our vision is replaced by loyalty to not upsetting the mob. After all, *they* might 'save' us by suddenly deciding to give our places of worship their support. But what would they be supporting?

Linking survival to numerical growth, such organisations pander to the whims of the age while forgetting the ancient task entrusted to our generation: the task of finding our commonality in the face of disparity and discord. Afraid that the secularised mass will feel further alienated by the use of religious language, the liberal religionist frequently thinks that by removing religious language from their vocabulary they will make what they represent more appealing. The result is a meaningless free for all, an anchorless voyage requiring no commitment or dedication, an a la carte spirituality that requires nothing from nobody because nothing is very important, a non conformity for non conformity's sake, an abdication of the call to search deeply for the meaning of our lives, even if that meaning is meaningless by its very nature.

The clear benefit of such religion is that it creates a place of comfort in a world that knows only too well how to reject. The disadvantage, however, is that we reduce religion to the lowest common denominator in order to avoid offence.

Instead of courageously and creatively using the tools we have inherited to dig deeply for what unites us, we offer a dull, yet sometimes dogmatic humanism, leaving the soul of humankind aching for the transcendence and mystery that may have sent it into a church in the first place. Thus the project of liberal religion becomes, ironically, not a celebration of the commonality that transcends our distinctive experiences, but a denial of the distinctiveness and commonality entirely. The adventure of faith becomes the duty to mark only our superficial sameness – not the sameness that might exist as the pinnacle of human experience, but the sameness that masquerades as something important when it is really nothing more than a mass denial of our individual and collective profundity. In this way the fundamental search for questions (never mind answers) which haunts every human life is rejected in favour of not rocking the boat. This appears to be the price of survival.

A religion embarked on such a course is doomed. Placing political correctness, group cohesion and corporate comfort before the experiences that send us into church in the first instance displays a singular lack of faith that something better may be found if we push off from the shore of our existential sleep. If liberal religious people want to take seriously the invitation to celebrate human commonality, as by and large they say they do, then there has to be an acknowledgement that the very commonality we treasure has not been found in the politically correct world of liberal religion as we have lived it for over a century. The equality agenda, which preoccupied us for decades, may have changed things for women and people of colour, but it has not changed the course of human history for the better. Our statute books are filled with legislation aimed at making society better for people, but people continue to suffer, and the perpetrators of offence suffer too as the projection of their self rejection goes unchallenged. Legislating for equality is not the same thing as changing hearts and minds. Telling a woman that she has the right to equal pay is not the same as respecting the endless value of her nature. Such an appreciation cannot be legislated for. It comes from a place far removed from the utilitarian world. It comes from the place religion is supposed to honour.

Maybe it's time to take a risk and trust that what is worth searching for is to be found in the sometimes uncomfortable world of our diversity, and not before, beside, or behind it. If the demands of political correctness have left us feeling isolated, if our fear of offending another has compounded our loneliness, then it may just be worth our while taking the risk of leaving our sparsely populated comfort zone, no matter how liberal it may be. It may be time to consider that the languages of the European religious traditions do not need to offend when they are set within the context of kindness and compassion.

The importance of holding onto language is apparent when we look at the annihilation of pagan vocabulary by the Christian Church. Rooted as it was in the cycles of nature, paganism had a natural respect for the planet which gives us a home. Its language empowered people to feel their natural connection to the earth, and from this sense of connection an ethic emerged that caused little damage to the land, sea and air. Christianity's very otherworldly approach divorced humankind from its environmental context. Its language of exploitation and dominance has had a clear impact on the health of the planet. Today the Christian Church struggles in trying to develop an ethic that might sustain the earth as a living sphere. It is interesting to think that the Church might well need to return to the traditions it destroyed in order to discover a more truthful understanding of the natural world. The power of its prophesy might well rely on the sincerity of its apology to the pagan dead.

Language, like most things, is evolutionary in nature. One of the tasks facing religious people today is to hold onto language while simultaneously allowing it to reveal new insight and guidance. Language can be like a lover: when we treat it well it responds in ways we could never have imagined. What we think we know can surprise us when we respect its inherent worth pre reflectively. To reject religious language is to reject a possible path to meaning in our lives. While religious language may have become soiled and degraded by right wing fanatics, it must be taken back and re examined for the meanings it might contain. The future of religion, I suspect, will have more to do with allowing our language to evolve new meanings and less to do with discarding what might appear, at first glance, to be difficult, outdated and offensive.

I have purposely painted this polarised picture for you because I want to highlight the beloved community as something fundamentally different in form from the flagrant individualism of the spirituality industry, different also from the religion which is offended by the human person, and different from the religion that is afraid of what we might call the depth and profundity of the spiritual experience, manifested in the rejection of its language. The starting point of beloved community is not to be found in a theology, in a person, or in a god. It is to be found wherever you are, whatever you are, whenever you are. Its starting point is in *our* experience of being human, cast upon the earth together, at this particular moment in time, with a fundamental need to find the hope that might sustain our lives.

The *Darkling Thrush*, which opened this chapter, was written as the nineteenth century gave way to the twentieth. Its author, Thomas Hardy, saw beyond the headstrong optimism of the Enlightenment mindset and felt the despondency that would later come to define the twentieth century. Yet, in the song of a fragile, 'blast beruffled bird' he detected an air of hope.

The contrast between overwhelming despair and fragile hope finds a natural home in the spiritual frame of mind where paradox and contrast are frequently relied upon as means of interpreting the world. Christianity's 'criminal' Christ, Buddhism's fat renunciate, Islam's wise fool all suggest that the knowledge sought by the spiritual seeker is not logical or even consistent. In fact Aristotelian logic and its many offspring frequently stand as obstacles to spiritual engagement. Like the Zen monks of the East and like the Rhineland mystics of the eleventh century, today's seeker repeatedly need to embrace the subtleties of paradox and pun to transcend the utilitarian language that maintains an unnecessary gap between the human subject and the mystery which can both haunt and console its days.

Hardy's detection of hope, therefore, is not to be understood as a calculated assessment of how the present will shape the future. It is, rather, to be appreciated as a fundamental cry of the soul. It is man learning from bird the paradoxical message that in the face of hopelessness there is always hope. It is man responding to the revelation of nature that despite the bleakness of the landscape before us, despondency can be transfigured by the feeble song of a bird.

From many perspectives our world looks bleak. War, hunger and environ mental catastrophe fill our newspapers each day. Dr Johnson's ability to fold his newspaper away before tucking into his favourite evening meal unperturbed would be seriously challenged in this day and age when the enormity of the problems facing our planet and its many creatures grow ever more apparent. Truly, if we are to be responsible human beings we can no longer ignore what is going on around us. Nor can we fall into the pit of inertia caused by despondency. We simply have to hope, understanding that hope cannot be calculated or planned. Hope is, rather, what we hold on to. It is the ground upon which we decide to stand. It is the hand that leads us into the world as active agents of change and not as passive victims of what might seem inevitable. A proper awareness of hope's dynamic quality invites us to move beyond the notion of spirituality as an exercise purely focused on interiority, and embrace instead the force, that while having great interior quality, links us to our fellows and to the cosmos in which we live. Hope reminds us that we are not here to merely survive. Life means more than survival, we must hope.

Chapter Three

Beloved Community – Hanging out in Postmodernity

THE last three hundred years have seen considerable improvement in how the human subject's autonomous value is honoured in large parts of the world. Universal suffrage, human rights, and regulations on work practice are all results of the major shift in consciousness ushered in during what we now call the Enlightenment. The Enlightenment's celebration of individual identity improved the quality of life for countless numbers of people, and its rationalism removed much of the superstition that had kept previous generations 'in their place.'

For Nietzsche (1844 1900) the Enlightenment was nevertheless a failure. As well as failing to move humankind towards knowledge that might free it, it had actually strengthened the fetters of enslavement by offering interpretations of our experience that were ultimately damaging. Enslavement was inevitable for the young German because Enlightenment models of interpretation upheld the view that history leads us towards total knowledge, and as long as humans accepted this idea they would be forced into playing second fiddle to the Absolute which would one day be revealed. As an antidote, Nietzsche offered us the *overman* (Übermensch): a vision of the autonomous human, free from all entanglements to so called higher causes. God was dead. It was impossible, therefore, to sin against him. The overman was the meaning of the earth, and the sin in Nietzsche's world was 'to esteem the entrails of the unknowable higher than the meaning of the earth...'[13] Despite Nietzsche's rejection of the Enlightenment models, this pre Freudian endorsement of what, for many, appears to be the ego centred human being is perhaps the peak of Enlightenment individualism and certainly the apex of Nietzsche's own search for freedom.

Notwithstanding widespread rejection of Nietzsche's overman, the evidence suggests it has been embraced at least partially. Wherever individual autonomy is placed before the collective good we see the overman in action. In Britain, the motoring lobby's use of human rights to undermine counter global warming measures is a classic example. The 2006 BBC television series, 'The Amazing Mrs Pritchard,' following the fortunes of a fictitious British prime minister, sees the protagonist pelted with eggs for introducing a weekly no car day. The culprit turns out to be a mother who objects to having to walk her children to school and sees such an inconvenience as a fundamental infringement of her human rights. There's a sense of poignancy in considering that while Nietzsche's speculation has contemplated the endless freedom of the human subject, it might well be the earth itself, and not the tyrant god he despised, which puts boundaries on such freedom.

Of all the tensions that beset the world of ethics and morality it is perhaps the friction between individual rights and the collective good that matters most. No one with a heart wants to see the human subject degraded and reduced in stature by the claims of the mob. However, if the twenty first century is teaching us anything it is that human well being relies on a delicate balance between individual autonomy and collective responsibility.

The American philosopher, Josiah Royce (1855 1916), set his mind to exploring this balance in the late nineteenth century. Royce was an immensely interesting man. A good friend of William James (they were friends despite a difference of opinion), a teacher of T S Eliot and a fine philosopher who is only now coming to be appreciated in his own right, Royce saw the shortcomings in Nietzsche's support of the individual's autonomous will and offered another vision. Whereas Nietzsche celebrated the ethic that springs from individual consciousness, Royce argued that consciousness is rooted in community and ethics must rise from there too. While remaining a true upholder of the Enlightenment's celebration of the individual's value, Royce understood this value to be, of necessity, rooted in community.

For Royce, the ethical vision of the individualist is doomed to failure precisely because of its individualism. 'There is only one way to be an ethical individual,' Royce wrote in his 1908 book, *The Philosophy Of*

Loyalty, and 'that is to choose your cause, and then to serve it, as the Samurai his feudal chief, as the ideal knight of romantic story his lady, in the spirit of all the loyal'.[14] The notion of loyalty is central to Royce's philosophy. Firstly, an individual must freely choose a cause and offer that cause loyalty. Secondly, as causes are not found wholly by introspection, but rather through our interactions with others, the community becomes the place where the cause is served. Community, then, is actually a source of consciousness. It is in community that we see the causes played out beyond the limitations of our own internal musings. In this sense, the community becomes the place (not necessarily a physical place) where the cause is served. Royce noted that communities that do wrong are focused on themselves. Our loyalty, according to Royce, should be to the vision. The community is the place in which it is set and through which it is lived. It is in community that we become interpreters and promoters of the vision. For this reason he went on to say 'My life means nothing, either theoretically or practically, unless I am a member of a community.'[15]

Royce was one of the first, if not *the* first, to use the term 'beloved community' to describe the form of human society that seeks to honour both individual identity and its collective context. We are perhaps more familiar with the term in relation to two great characters of twentieth century religion, Dr Martin Luther King and Fr Henri Nouwen. They both dedicated their lives to raising our awareness of the impulse that binds people together, despite race, disability and creed. This impulse was based on the infinite worth of the human subject, but unlike Nietzsche, they saw this worth as the very foundation of a better society and not as an invitation to go it alone. In both their projects, an appreciation of our own value liberates us to appreciate that value in others. Speaking from a Christian perspective, like Royce, they saw the reality of God's love for us as an invitation to contemplate God's love for all people. The Kingdom of God became for them a place defined by this truth. All ethics, morality, speculation, metaphysics and doctrine were secondary to the reality of human belovedness. No wonder both were viewed with suspicion by the institutions that claimed them.

For those of us exploring these themes from non Christian, post Christian or atheistic backgrounds, the language of King and Nouwen does not have to be off putting. After all, the presence of love as a basic value in our experience is not an insight of religion alone. It is perhaps best described as an anthropological part of everyone. If we close our mouths long enough and listen and watch the world around us, we realise that we are part of a universe of tremendous scale. To say simply that we are part of it is just an extraordinary thing to say. But then another extraordinary insight follows: these other creatures, these women and men who dance, jump, walk, run, crawl and sail through life are also part of it. In such moments words fail us and we are overcome by the sense of just how magnificent all life is, from the chalk marks of the greatest mathematician on the blackboard to the struggle of the slug in the garden, trying his best to get to the cabbage leaf before the blackbird gets to him. Our experiences of love are experiences of nature at its very deepest and most precious – when we feel a part of it, part of the dust on the outmost rings of the expanding universe and part of the pavement on which we stand. It can be as if nature collides with mystery and beauty and suddenly the bastard at the end of the street becomes my brother, for whom this entire universe has been created. It can be as if the television evangelist in the white suit, telling people that they are doomed without the saving blood of the lamb becomes my brother and his over made up wife becomes my sister. In moments like these our beliefs are unimportant and only the fact that we do believe remains, only the fact that we are all here, trying our best to believe in something, even if it is only that our freedom might be found in the bottom of a bottle. No philosophy, no theology and no science has ever come close to describing the quality of consciousness that makes us feel connected to other human beings when we may have many reasons not to.

The problem with religion is that it wants to take this experience and explain it away in terms of doctrine. It is never enough that we feel it. It has to be battered and built into epistemology. When religion views itself as the guardian of epistemology, when it insists on a marriage between mystery and metaphysics, then devotion to mystery gives way to the demands of dogma, and division is the inevitable outcome. Perhaps the greatest lie of religion is the lie that epistemology is supremely important. As long as religion continues to insist that it is, its ability to help us live with the many contradictions of life is seriously undermined.

One thing we can be sure of is that politics and philosophy are preoccupied with the same epistemological concern. As if a human being didn't have enough problems by virtue of their ambiguous nature, they must also face the prospect of additional corporate conflict caused by the war of ideas which hopes to one day crown a system of knowing. The problems in our world are exacerbated not by the psychopaths who seek to cause havoc, but by people who genuinely wish to cause no harm, but who cannot find a common ground on which to stand with those who entertain different interpretations of the world. Religionists, politicians and thinkers maybe have to grasp the simple fact that beyond all the differences of opinion, custom and dress, there is the reality of human sameness – all of us here, coming from a common place, even if we can't agree where it is, and heading towards a common destiny. If liberal religion is to have a future it has to grasp the subtleties of this discussion and discover a way of being in the world that embodies the qualities of the future we are hoping to create.

Such a future cannot be built from scratch, but has to acknowledge the past from which the future will arise. The history of liberal religious organisations is submerged in the attempt to make religion compatible with the insights of Enlighten ment philosophy. The Enlightenment is recognisable by its insistence that truth is more closely linked to rationalism than it is to myth, tradition or religious authority. While the chasm between the philo sophical idealism of Kant and the empiricism of Hume is indeed a wide one, they share a common Enlightenment presumption that the start and end of philosophy is located in the rational faculty of humankind.

A major shortcoming of liberal religion today is that it continues to locate the search for truth in the rational faculty and not in the totality of the human experience, which includes our *meta rational* experience of otherness, nature and mystery. One wonders just how long the rational loving world of liberal religion has to remain an extraneous activity before we realise that rationalism cannot describe, never mind explain, the sum of human experience. There are aspects of human living which, while certainly not irrational, cannot lend themselves to rational inquiry, perhaps because their source is not rational.

The debate is the basic tool of the rational search, because rationalism promotes the notion that ideas must collide with each other in order for a chastened victor to emerge. The philosophical materialists who used Hegel (1770 1831) to explain the mechanism by which humankind progressed promoted his conflict of ideas (dialectics) to make their point. However, Hegel's re evaluation of Immanuel Kant's idealism is more complex and profound. Hegel's positing of Absolutes makes philosophy speculative and not dialectical, and we should never forget Hegel's attempts to locate the non rational into his overall system of philosophy. The Enlightenment was built

on deism, not atheism after all.[16]   This
is really just an aside, and one that is likely
to get me into trouble. The more
important point is that dialectics, as a
predictable mechanism, has emerged as the
fundamental way in which we understand
the evolution of ideas. Given, however, the
negative effect dialectics has had on our
world – over 250 wars in the twentieth
century for starters – it is worth
considering whether there is any hope of
refining the dialectic.

I have purposely used the word 'refine'
because there would be little sense in
arguing for the annihilation of the dialectic
process. The very fact that I am here
locked in a dialectic wrangle with dialectics
suggests it is impossible to do so. I
suspect Hegel was right when he suggested
consciousness relies on contrast.
However, all too often the patriarchal
systems at play in our societies have seen
conflict as an inevitable outcome of this
contrast. The results of this approach have
damaged us all.[17]

We have already observed what might
be called the spiritual experience, that
sense of being connected to the universe
and to the other creatures who populate it.

Those who have experienced such oneness are universal in their rejection of dialectics as a way to interpret the experience. Their poems and prayers and essays do not describe a state of uncompromising knowledge that seeks to battle it out with any opposing point of view. Rather, they describe a state of openness to life, an openness characterised by compassion for other people, who are each trying their best to come to terms with what this life may mean. In this context, being my brother's keeper has more to do with honouring my brother's experience and less to do with trying to interpret it for him. Epistemology gives way to care.

Putting ideas into conflict with one another, having blind faith that reason can grasp and solve the human predicament, promoting the notion that we are advancing down the road of history owing to the objective consistency of ideas – these are, perhaps, the most obvious shortcomings of the dialectic process. Liberal religion is in a unique position to offer an alternative. Free as it is from the totalitarianism of feeling itself superior, it can speak from its faith in the endless value of humankind to refine the dialectic.

By locating the categorical imperative in the totality of the human condition, liberal religion gives birth to the dialogical alternative. If dialectics is defined by its propensity for putting ideas into conflict with one another, then its dialogical counterpart is recognisable by the emphasis it places on the over arching mystery that gives rise to the ideas in the first place. If dialectics places its trust in the power of reason to knock these ideas into shape, then dialogue affirms that we shall never have the full picture and that speculation should never be the source of violence, hatred or revenge. If dialectics believes it can advance on the road of progress due to the objective consistency of ideas, then dialogue says we can stop and grow deeper due to the subjective profundity of the human being. If dialectics loves the logos, then dialogue loves the mysterious truth that transcends it. Beloved community relies on the art of dialogue to establish and sustain itself.

Reason is not the enemy in the beloved community. In fact reason is a beautiful thing, a necessary thing if we are to avoid falling into the pit of religious absolutism. It is how we understand and use it that should lend itself to scrutiny. Reason has never wiped a tear, held a hand or embraced the lonely. It has never painted a sunset, written a good poem or rolled a craved for cigarette. It has, however, laid the foundations for more justice and equity in human affairs. It has held psychotic men accountable for their actions and brought tyrannies to an end. There is much to fear about living in an unreasonable world. However, reason works best when it lives in relation to the poetic, intuitive and mysterious dimensions of our lives. It is done a great disservice when dogmatic materialists use it to deny the importance of the poetic, intuitive and mysterious in our experience.

Whenever people meet there will inevitably be an exchange of ideas, for consciousness lives itself out through ideas. However, when ideas are shared in the beloved community, they are shared in the knowledge that our insights are only ever partial and shrouded in a mystery that extends, and perhaps even transcends, the limits of our intellects. In this sense the beloved community becomes a place concerned with encountering the totality of the human subject, even when we cannot fathom what that totality entails.

Chapter Four

The Mystery in Humanity

WE ALL encounter people who feel the presence of depth and mystery in their lives. These same people are confronted with a plethora of religions that want to convert that sense of mystery into doctrinal belief systems. Such a habit on the part of religion is off putting and does nothing more than generate alienation in the many people seeking to explore the character of their experience. Perhaps more worryingly, the reluctance on the part of many religions to live with mystery results in forms of thinking that are ultimately unable to engage with the complexity of life and the problems which this complexity engender. While some of the greatest seers have understood the essentially simple nature of a healthy life, they have simultaneously eschewed the simplistic interpretations upheld by sadly too many religious institutions. When religions decide to ignore the complex in favour of the simplistic, they make themselves little more than hiding places for those not willing to think.

These hiding places are characterised by rigid and dogmatic explanations of the world. Instead of embracing the puzzling, peculiar and weird as aspects of life which lend themselves to our imaginations and intellects, the hiding place offers belief in fairies as the antidote to our lack of knowledge. When mystery is embraced it is used only to uphold first principles from which the rest of the fairytales can be expounded. Mystery, in this sense, becomes the enemy of anyone interested in looking for the truth.

Why do the religious hiding places in postmodernity only use mystery to uphold certainty in the face of overwhelming uncertainty? The answer, I suspect, has something to do with the fear we feel when we allow ourselves to experience our ignorance. After all, there is a level of comfort in thinking that there is some big father figure who cares and intervenes to make things better for us. The twentieth century, however, makes such belief suspect. We know that millions of people can die and God does not intervene. We know that the huts of death camps can be filled with the hum of intercessions, often selfless in content, and Big Daddy in Heaven does nothing. To insist that in some 'mysterious' way God can, or does intervene, sixty years after the Shoah, sends God into an ultimately secluded, neurotic and extraneous realm where most people are not willing to go.

Mystery does not exist to fill the gaps left by our partial understandings. Rather, mystery is linked to the compulsion we can all feel to recognise the intrinsic infinitude of all things. Mystery is a falling to our knees in the face of the indescribable.

Healthy religion does not need to be linked with theism. It needs to be linked with our experience of mystery and we need to create new relationships which allow the experience of mystery to be articulated and shared in such a way that it emboldens us to be prophetic voices in our world. Most contemporary theology is by and large a futile pastime because it refuses to accept this fact. Instead, it insists on having first hand knowledge of what God wants. This knowledge is referred to as revelation.

Within Protestantism, these claims are supported by belief in the Bible as the revealed word of God, while Catholicism is more likely to use tradition to support its claims. Both approaches amount to the same thing: they imprison love in a past that holds little hope for the present or future. When examined on a purely logical basis they both come close to constituting acts of idolatry given that they place a collection of words before the force and power of the love which most of them claim they are trying to promote. Liberal religion has been reticent about making such claims because it has denied the idea that religion is fundamentally about revelation. Instead it has focused on religion's capacity to help others. In this way theology has been replaced by social ethics in the liberal tradition. But, and it is a big but, we don't have to be religious to help others. Altruism is not the reserve of the religious. Perhaps liberal religion has to re embrace the notion of revelation and acknowledge the great questions that occasionally wake us from the slumber in which we conduct our day to day lives and asks us what is this life all about? Does it have meaning? If it doesn't have meaning what might that meaninglessness mean?

Unlike previous generations we have the hindsight to understand that the human condition is the primary revelation we have. Historical and literary criticism of the Bible makes it plain for all to see that, at best, it's a commentary of humanity's attempt to understand. When tradition is held accountable by the forces of historical methodology we find that frequently it has been nothing more than an attempt to maintain power structures and monopolies. Yet despite all this we are still left wondering, not what the answer is, but what the question might be that helps us move beyond the anxiety of not knowing.

The more stories I hear in my vestry about this very issue, the more I am inclined to think that revelation is primarily rooted in our interactions with others. Before there were scriptures and traditions there were people, and what is deepest and most profound about our lives lived itself out through their experiences. Today that revelation is still at play. The most important lessons we can learn are often learnt from our dealings with other people. In this sense life itself is the primary revelation. We may want to be overmen, focused only on our own drives and desires, or we may just want to succumb to some system that allows us not to think. However, revelation continues to knock on the door through the experience of living with other people, and through our attempts to love others and be loved by them.

Preachers and poets throw the word 'love' around quite a lot and it's worth considering for a moment what I mean when I use it. We live in an age that has come to define love often in terms of emotional pleasure. Sometimes love in this sense means no more than dependency and when the emotional pleasure ends or temporarily stops the love is said to be gone. I do not seek to deny the strong emotional aspects of loving; however, I'm more interested in the notion of love as a sense of concerned connectedness for another. I'm interested in the unspeakable aspect of love which transcends the emotional and which is intuitive more than it is cerebral. Love is in some way related to trust. While life teaches us that we cannot always trust in the goodness of other people, we can at least trust in the struggle we all share by virtue of being alive. We can trust in our common humanity, contradictory and troubling as it may be. Love in this sense is not about emotional satisfaction or gratification. It is nothing less than allowing ourselves to live from that graceful place where our common humanity is apparent. I have come to conclude that this is the only way in which we can love our enemies, and it is the only hope we have of our enemies loving us.

Enhancing the quality of this love within the world generally, and within our liberal religious communities specifically, is solely dependent on our openness to grace. In the same way that you can't sink a rainbow, you cannot legislate for intimacy and love. Those who claim you can are wrong. We cannot legislate for love because love is not a human construct. Despite what a Freudian or Post Freudian might tell you, its source lies not in our need or in our backgrounds or in our fears. Love was born among the gods and the poems and prayers of the world's religious traditions remind us that we do not create it. It is, rather, revealed to us as an invitation to acknowledge that we are linked in a most sublime way to other people, to the cosmos and to the mystery which envelops both. The invitation is not only to acknowledge this singular fact, but to actually embrace it and begin the process of living from it. If celebrating and exploring this deeply [extra]ordinary experience is not our vocation as religious people, then what is?

I have drawn a conclusion from my short time in ministry, that most people who come to me for advice or just to share a burden are not, as is commonly thought, depressed, but rather anxious. I cannot make this claim in terms of a clinical diagnosis because I am not qualified to do so, but the overriding feeling they carry seems to be that of worry and not sadness. Maybe this speaks to our own experience. Maybe we spend a lot of our time worried, and at times our anxiety is compounded by the worry that something bigger to worry about is surely just around the corner. I sometimes suspect that this anxiety is based largely on the sheer obscurity and vagueness of self identity. We look at the religions of the world and get an idea of what they have to offer, but we are ultimately in a place where we do not know what we want. The purveyors of spiritual insight are everywhere in the twenty first century. It may be that we

have tried many of their delights, but
ultimately found ourselves back in our
Tracey Emin type beds, the contents of
our postmodern lives scattered around us,
wondering if there is in fact a piece of
knowledge that might just set us free.

The knowledge that sets people free is
what religious people call revelation. For
the Christian, freedom is found in the
incarnation of the Christ as set out in the
New Testament. In Islam it is found by
following the laws given to Mohammad
(PBUH) from God via the angel Gabriel
and found today in the Holy Koran. For
Hindus freedom lies at some point in the
future when the karmic cycle comes to an
end through the practice of yogic
disciplines found in the Vedic texts.
Science, which for all its scepticism looks
set to become more religious like in
appearance as the Richard Dawkins speak
from their dogmatic chairs, is certainly not
immune from the freedom bug either,
given the scientists who look forward to
the day when they will have the knowledge
that makes sense of the world entirely. At
times these differing approaches go to war
with each other making some of us wonder
whether it would be better to try to free

ourselves from our pursuit of freedom altogether!

The search for freedom has become yet another burden for the postmodern man and woman. In this sense, the anxiety I encounter in the vestry and for matter in my own life can be understood as an response to the suspicion that the truth that sets us free can never be discovered in a world filled with an almost infinite amount of choice. In such a world epistemology is at least difficult, perhaps at most impossible. If this is indeed the nature of the condition, then it may be worth our while re imaging revelation as the thing that actually points us towards a way of living authentically in the company of our doubts.

This takes us into one of the most controversial areas of contemporary philosophical discourse. Richard Wolin, in his recent book *The Seduction of Unreason*,[18] quite rightly draws our attention to the company that philosophical ideas keep. He highlights the distinction between philosophies that reject epistemology and philosophies that state all ethics must be based on epistemological insight. More specifically he highlights how wrong politics can be when it divorces itself from the philosophical foundations on which morality can be built. Nietzsche and Heidegger's assertion that man is the measure of all things, and their attack on the broader assumptions of rationalism, lead ultimately to a world where politics is just another choice and not the manifestation of thought out conviction.

Framing the situation thus, Wolin presents us with an either/or situation. Either we accept the universe as a morally empty place and live with the consequences, or we assert that there are universal truths which provide a moral framework within which to live. The beloved community accepts the paradox that while universals are present, our ability to grasp them is limited. In this sense the beloved community is a place where solidarity is forged as a basic support in each other's search for the elusive universals, and a place where compassion is generated for each other as we struggle on such this search. However, the journey cannot end here.

The clash between universal and subjective notions of truth is one of the most serious threats facing the human race today. On a global scale, the strength of religions that insist on their ability to grasp the universals is at the heart of many conflicts with what they perceive to be morally redundant and degenerate secularists. In society more generally, those who uphold the quagmire of subjectivity seem to offer little hope that we can find unity and common purpose as we look into a world requiring unified and common approaches to heal the many divisions that make life so difficult for countless numbers of people. It is possible for those of us with no particular philosophical axe to grind to see the truth in both positions. As characters living in history we have knowledge of what a world without rigorous universal truth looks like. It is the world of the Nazi, based solely on the pragmatism of upholding one's particular convictions irrespective of the integrity of those convictions. In such a self centred world we need only justify our actions to ourselves.

Ironically, in its flight from universal truths the Nazi party invented other ones, far more damaging in fact. The paradoxical truth at the heart of this modern/postmodern debate is that the assertion that there is no universal truth is itself a universal statement, and the contention that there is, a subjective one. Totalitarianism is easily reached from both starting points. If we could take this clash out of the dialectic it has become embroiled in, we might see that universal truth and individual interpretation work best when they are in symbiotic relation to each other. It is not a case of either/or. It is a case of both.

In a religious sense the role of mystery is an important aid in developing such a symbiotic relationship and the biblical tale of Sodom illustrates this point well. Derrick Sherwin Bailey's pioneering work in the 1950s drew attention to the word upon which the entire interpretation of the narrative rests, the Hebrew verb to *know*.[19] When the men of the city came to Lot's house and said they wanted to know Lot's visitors, this was the word they used.

I was astonished to learn that this verb, *yadha*, occurs 943 times in the Jewish Bible and on only ten occasions does it refer unambiguously to carnal knowledge.[20] I began to wonder why people assumed that the men of the city wanted to know Lot's visitors carnally?

This assumption, made by many writers over the years, is seriously undermined when we consider the risks involved in having strangers inside the city's walls after dark without the elders' permission. Was it not more likely that the men of the city wanted to know who the strangers were so they could sleep secure in their beds that night?

When we look at other areas of the Bible where the story of Sodom was mentioned we discovered the interesting fact that none of the other biblical writers refer to the sin of Sodom in the context of sex. Isaiah and Jeremiah refer to the sin of Sodom as being concerned with inhospitality to strangers. On the one occasion when Jesus refers to it in Matthew's gospel he condemns the city for being inhospitable to angelic visitors.[21] When I spoke to a rabbi he told me that Jews don't see the sin of Sodom in the context of sex, but in the context of Jewish hospitality codes. What becomes apparent to us is that this story is preoccupied with a theme that runs powerfully throughout the Jewish scriptures – God calls on us to welcome others that come our way.

The notion of welcome is an indisputable theme in the story, even for those who claim its real import lies elsewhere. But who exactly should we be welcoming? You may recall that the visitors in Lot's house are angels. Now eight foot tall cherubs with the bodies of Adonis and the wings of a swan are not easy for some of us to swallow. But the angel is such a familiar character, not only in the Judaeo Christian tradition, but in almost every religious tradition, that it deserves some consideration.

The angel is a messenger shrouded in mystery. It is never predictable in the sense that we know what it is up to. As Jacob found to his ultimate benefit, an angel is quite likely to act erratically in order to effect the change it desires. However, the message this mysterious character brings always has some importance attached to it, and, though we may not be aware of its meaning, its place in the overall scheme of things usually becomes apparent. In this context the angel, far from being a mere sign of superstition and fancy, is in fact a metaphor for the people, places and situations that point us towards the universals which haunt the shortcomings of human society. To accept the angel of mystery as part of our lives is to accept that universal truth is constantly at work in our world, even when we do not recognise it. To accept mystery is to accept that despite our ignorance life has a sacred import, which even when it is unknown is nevertheless present. To accept mystery in this sense is to accept the symbiosis of universal truth and subjective interpretation

The fact is we do not need to know the truth in order to build a loving and just society. We need only be in touch with the mystery that surrounds the truth to know that love is better than hate, that peace is better than war, that kindness is better than cruelty, and that human community is better than isolation. By allowing universal truth a symbiotic relationship with individual interpretation we establish the necessary safeguards against the nihilism that our world cannot sustain, while at the same time encouraging all people to use, in the words of George Kimmich Beach, their 'finite freedom well.'[22] If the postmodern religious search is ultimately a search for ways of living together with doubt, then a reconnecting with mystery might well be the foremost feature of the terrain we seek.

The canon of the beloved community then is the canon of our experience, shared with each other. Its Old Testament is the tragedy of sectarian religion. Its New Testament the promise that the mystery of life is a strong enough foundation on which to build a world with more justice, hope and love in it. Those who reject the Bible as the revealed word of God need not be impoverished by the absence of a scriptural revelation. They need only recognise that revelation is living itself out in their own lives, and in the lives of the people they live with, and in the life of the planet they live on.

The issue of revelation is always tied to the issue of authority. Religions use their revelations as sources of authority not only in terms of their internal systems of governance, but in terms of their relationships to the wider world as well. James Martineau, perhaps the leading light of liberal religion in Britain and Ireland in the nineteenth century, examined the notion of authority in a religious system that did not place its absolute trust in the Bible. While the issue had featured in his work for some considerable period, it was the twilight of his life that gave us *The Seat of Authority* (1890).[23] The book marks a pivotal moment in the history of liberal religion this side of the Atlantic. Whereas his religious forbearers, such as Lindsay, Priestley and Belsham, had sought consistency between their rational dispositions and the truth claims of the Bible, Martineau allowed the conclusions of literary and historical critique to undermine the Bible as an objective authority altogether. Literary and historical inconsistency married to a low Christology — he saw Jesus as an example to follow and not as God to be worshipped — enabled Martineau not only to put forward, but actually to celebrate the conscientious reason of humankind as the final seat of authority. His conclusions were very much based on the Enlightenment model of the autonomous self and they have been appreciated by every theologian facing a magisterial firing squad ever since.[24] However, if the religious search of postmodernity is concerned with marrying collective doubt to collective identity in a way that fosters a more just and equitable world, then Martineau's conclusions have to be set in a creative tension with the idea of commonality. In other words, while celebrating the role of the conscience, we have to explore the ways in which conscience lives in relationship to otherness. Such an exploration involves examining the dynamics at play when we accept the revelatory significance of other people. These dynamics will be the focus of the next chapter.

Chapter Five

The Comfort and Challenge of Community

I ONCE heard the story of a young seminarian who was very impressed by the spiritual depth and insight of an older priest. Deciding that this priest would make an ideal confessor, the seminarian called him to arrange a meeting. The priest generously told the lad to come over straight away, and within an hour they were sitting face to face.

Just when the seminarian thought the time had come to begin his confession, the priest suggested that there were a few things he should know. What followed was a thirty minute confession from the priest. Every vow he had broken, every woman he had loved, every hate he had ever entertained was shared with the young man. When the priest had finished he looked at his guest and said, 'Now I can be your confessor.'[25]

Revelation is the discourse that speaks to the heart of humankind. The revelation

we offer to each other in the beloved
community is not the revelation of the
saved. It is the revelation of the lost. The
fact is that many of us are walking around
pretending that everything is fine,
pretending that we've got it sorted,
pretending that life makes sense to us
somehow. In this way we enable and
empower the panoptical discourse. The
pretension can be so convincing that we
even manage to convince ourselves for
some of the time. The pressures to pretend
are everywhere in evidence. Polite society
doesn't admire tales of our inner conflicts.
Try explaining to a prospective employer
that you occasionally find the world so
depressing that you like to stay in bed, and
you'll see how far you get. Staying in bed
is for Saturdays, and even then, only for
some.

The most generous thing we can do in
this context is to share with those who
come to us with their struggles just how
lost we ourselves are. By sharing the ways
in which we fail, the panoptical discourse
itself diminishes in strength, because we
learn of the many ways in which it fails us.
The panoptical discourse fails to control us
when we recognise that there is another

discourse tapping at the deepest part of ourselves, the part some people call soul. It is the discourse that says maybe there is more to life. It is the discourse that says maybe you are not alone. Because it honours the 'maybe' it can take you from the cell of your alienation and place you in a family we call humanity where others may be asking the same questions. If they are asking these questions, they are undermining the discourse which has forbidden you from contemplating a world beyond the Panopticon. The experiences that led to the questions become the stuff of revelation because they reveal to you the ways in which your humanity is diminished by unquestionably accepting the discourse you were given. In this way we can understand the beloved community to be primarily a community of brokenness – none of us quite fitting in to the straightjacket they call 'normality.'

In this community certain dynamics will be at play, which, if understood correctly, can open doors we never even knew existed. These dynamics are to do with the ways in which we understand the other people who populate our lives. As sources of revelation they deserve particular attention, as does our response to them. I'm going to give three examples: the friend, the foe and the fool.

The Buddhists have a concept of the kalyana mitra, the noble friend, which John O'Donohue equates with the old Celtic notion of the anam cara, the soul friend.[26] Just as the anam cara is a person with whom you can be completely honest, the kalyana mitra is a person who can give us a perspective on our lives which we might be blinded to ourselves. The kalyana mitra is not concerned with how much money you're making, or how your career is going, or where you're going on holiday. Rather they are concerned with how your outer life in the world is reflecting the stirrings in the deepest part of you, a part which some people call soul.

We can of course pick our friends, and usually, unless we have strong sadistic tendencies, we choose people we like, we choose people who like us, people with similar interests and so on. But often where the kalyana mitra is concerned it can be as if they have been chosen for us. It can be as if there is a great magnet in the person; we are drawn to them and linked to them in ways we perhaps don't understand.

Conversation with these people is never dull. It may not even be polite because there can be impatience to get to the important matters. No compliments, no how is you father, no where did you get that top. Instead there is a hunger to share the latest movements in that deep part of ourselves which we don't like to talk about in polite company.

If morality is about doing what society says we should do, then frequently morality is absent from such conversations. Instead, the full force of our humanity is unleashed and the other person knows how to hold it. Whatever we tell them, their responses always remind us that we are still within the family of humanity, still deserving of love because we are human.

Religious people need these friendships particularly because of their propensity to form vanguards of morality around themselves. Such vanguards are related to the terrifying shadows which the upholders of overly strict moral systems often do not want to admit are there. These shadows can lead us into all sorts of dangerous behaviours. Unless we have people in our lives who know exactly how broken and messed up we are, we run the risk of harming both ourselves and others in our attempts to ignore the shadows.

When we come away from encounters with our soul friends we sometimes recognise that some new insight has been gained, some new depth plunged, some old fear has been understood. We may not know what time it is, but we know we have been touched by the extraordinary capacity of human interaction.

We might think that life would be smooth if we could spend it with our friends, or with our soul friend entirely. Not only is this practically impossible, it would also mean distancing ourselves from the revelations that are carried by our foes. We might hate admitting to it, but some of the most important lessons we learn come from those we do not like, and who sometimes do not like us. These lessons can be quite superficial in nature, like, for instance, our desire not to repeat behaviour we find objectionable in our enemies. However, sometimes the very presence of these people highlights aspects of our selves which we wish were not there. For every decent, kind, engaging individual, there is someone who can turn them into a tempestuous wreck in minutes.

I'll never forget the day one of my friends took to hiding behind the sofa to avoid someone they disliked and when the person had gone they emerged full of bitterness and hate. In every other situation this person was kind and considerate, but the presence of their enemy raised a sort of madness.

What's often at play here is what psychologists call projection. We encounter a person who embodies all that we hate and we react to it because what we hate is at play within ourselves. It is one of the greatest and hardest to accept ironies of living that those we want to reject most emphatically are those who hold the most important lessons we can learn. By accepting the importance of the foe, the beloved community becomes the place where the conflict experienced between foes is seen as something creative and necessary. In this way the invitation to love our enemies takes on a new meaning because to love our enemies is to be grateful to them, even when we don't want to be, for pointing out the ways in which we are enslaved.

There's a growing body of scholarship in Judaism and Christianity that links the idea of revelation with the fool.[27] When discussing with friends, someone reminded me that in Shakespeare's *King Lear* the fool is the only one able to tell the King the truth, suggesting that the Talmudic advice, to recognise your folly is the first step towards wisdom, has, at least, some truth in it.

Nasruddin, a mysterious character, perhaps from the thirteenth century Middle East, is commonly identified as a wise fool. Stories about him abound from Turkey to Afghanistan to Iran. On a superficial level the stories are simple and funny. But if you pay a bit more attention you may notice the sublime at play in the tales. In terms of our own examination of the panoptical discourse there's a particular story that has, perhaps, more than a little pertinence:

Nasruddin, we are told, had a high regard for his donkey. One day the townspeople came running, 'Nasruddin, your little donkey is lost!' Nasruddin replied, 'Praise be to God! If I was on him I would have been lost too!'[28]

The relationship between foolishness and wisdom is further underlined by even the most cursory glance into the world of the comic. Tommy Cooper didn't even need words to make us laugh. Every week he climbed onto a stage and showed us how funny it can be to fail. We laughed, perhaps, because we know what it's like to be portraying success in this world of ours. We laughed because we know what it's like to smile broadly at those around us while feeling the ground moving under our feet.

I don't know how many times I have been convinced of a theory that explains why I am the way I am, only to discover, after some time, another theory that explains it more accurately. The friend, the foe and the fool, when listened to respectfully, can draw attention away from the most recent theory or concept, and cause us to attend instead to the continuous and gradual unveiling of our natures, and they can do this not because they are consciously wise or expert human development professionals. They can do this because providence is at work in human interaction. This was why the writer of the Letter of James told the early Christians to confess their faults to one another.[29] He wasn't a Trisha or Oprah type character who was excited by group confessions. Rather, he grasped that when we are honest about just how lost we are, we learn to move beyond the often ego centred self improvement programme, and embrace instead the place of mystery in our lives. In other words no theory or concept can ever explain fully who we are. The presence of our self help theories about ourselves can, like the certainties of dogma, be a screen to shield us from our sheer ignorance about ourselves. Allowing mystery its place in our lives sends a powerful message to our egos that we are not fully in charge of who we are, and it's liberating to know we are not supposed to be.

Opening ourselves to the possibility that other people in our lives carry revelations for us can liberate us to be more attentive to those others in our lives. However, perhaps a word of warning is called for. Sigmund Freud noted a certain resistance in his patients when it came to wanting to know about themselves.[30] He noted that on some levels forces are at play which shun the self knowledge we think we are seeking. To overcome these forces, Freud developed the practice of free association. 'Instead of urging the patient to say something upon some particular subject, I now asked him to abandon himself to a process of free association – that is to say whatever came into his head, while ceasing to give any direction to his thoughts.'[31]

Freud's insight is a reminder that there is within all of us an urge not to know. There is something at play in all of us that rejects revelation. If you ever sit down with a therapist you will probably learn that you spend a lot of time skirting around issues and a lot of money trying to stay far away from some of the more difficult aspects of ourselves. I used to be annoyed at myself for doing it, but I get less annoyed now because I see it as an essential part of the process. It is essential because there is nothing as off putting as the razor of over analysis which forces people to come clean about themselves. That simply does not work. The non judgmental and creative nature of free association has much to teach religious people about how to handle the revelation of ourselves and others. It suggests that the knowledge we need most comes to us when we stop trying to control it.

Given the sensitive nature this process, it is important to have overarching principles that protect us from feeling overwhelmed by the whole thing. One of these principles has to be humour. Grounding as it does our flightiness and propensity to feel disconnected, humour can put things in perspective. Another principle is to be found in a sermon preached by one of the great exponents of liberal theology, Paul Tillich. Tillich examined our experience of alienation and the effect this has on our relationships. 'The depth of our separation lies in just the fact that we are not capable of a great and merciful divine love towards ourselves. We are separated from the mystery, the depth and the greatness of our existence.'[32]

Now I happen to think that's a pretty good summary of our condition, but Tillich doesn't stop at giving us a summary. He goes on to say, 'When the old compulsions reign within us as they have for decades, when despair destroys all joy and courage, sometimes at that moment a wave of light breaks into our darkness, and it is as though a voice were saying: You are accepted. You are accepted.'[33]

We all sometimes wish for a better life, a more popular personality, a more respectable occupation, but despite spending thousands of pounds on them, I still have the imperfections I had when I started to pay attention to myself. Perhaps the most difficult message for us to grasp is the message that the most profound change human beings can effect is a change in how we understand our imperfections. Our imperfections are not mere aberrations from some perceived sense of a normal life. They are part of a normal life. We can choose to see our imperfections as walls which prevent the light of Divine Love from shining on our darkness, or we can develop new relationships with them. We can learn to see them as the cracks through which the gods enter[34] – and this change is impossible without cultivating a 'merciful and divine love towards ourselves.'

I will never know fully why I am the way I am, but I can choose to spend my life crawling through the desert feeling sorry about it, or I can respond to the revelations in the people around me and cultivate a merciful and divine love towards myself and other people.

In order to do this we need to examine more closely a paradox at the heart of human life, a paradox which, if embraced, allows us to be in touch with more of our humanity that we commonly are. The precise nature of this paradox will be explored in the next chapter.

Chapter Six

The paradox of every life

THE problem with other people is that so many of them lack perfection! Building community with others would be easier if so and so were not around. I would find it so much easier if that person wasn't constantly getting on my nerves. We all learn just how irrational we are when it comes to the annoying people in our lives. For every well balanced, kind and entertaining person in the world there's a twit who can press buttons that turn them into neurotic savages.

It's not always easy to reconcile the notion of spirituality with imperfection. In the last chapter we contemplated the idea that we need to incorporate our imperfections into how we understand ourselves and others. The search is on, therefore, for something that helps us to do this.

There is a glaring paradox in all our lives. It is the paradox that everything we might ever need we already have, while at the same time we are poor, wanting and in need. We learn to deal with difficult people more effectively when we understand that this is a paradox contradicting the consistency of every life.

Fred Bratman was a secular Jewish friend of the Roman Catholic priest, Henri Nouwen. Their friendship had been ignited when the newspaper he worked for sent him to interview Henri for a special features column. Some years after their initial meeting, Fred asked Henri to write a book about his vision for the large mass of secular people who did not share his language and tradition. Henri's response was a book, *Life of the Beloved*. At the start of that book he recalls the story of the voice from heaven speaking after the baptism of the Christ. He writes,

I have been wondering if there might be one word I would most want you to remember when you finished reading all I wish to say. ... that special word has gradually emerged from the depths of my own heart. It is the word 'Beloved.' ...Being a Christian I first learned this word from the story of the baptism of Jesus of Nazareth. 'No sooner had Jesus come up out of the water than he saw the heavens torn apart and the Spirit, like a dove, descending on him. And a voice came from heaven: 'You are my Son, the Beloved; ...' The words, 'You are my Beloved' reveal the most intimate truth about all human beings, whether they belong to any particular tradition or not. Fred, all I want to say to you is 'You are the Beloved.' ... My only desire is to make these words reverberate in every corner or your being — 'You are the Beloved.'[35]

We, of course, live in a world where there are many voices telling us we are anything but the beloved. In fact much of what passes for Christian theology is based on the rather damaging notion that we are stained with original sin. In the secular world, despite its apparent rejection of Christianity, the tendency to denigrate and demean human existence still persists. This denigration is frequently upheld by the Panopticon, where, as we have already observed, only a fraction of our humanity is welcomed. To belong in such a society demands that we hide large swaths of who we are in the interests of manners and propriety. Repression and denial of our humanity are valued above and beyond any attempts to speak the truth. In such a culture people live in fear that their true selves might be seen, or perhaps it would be more correct to say their truer selves. The voice of twenty first century mainstream culture is one that encourages us to be only fractions of the people we are. So adept have these cultural forces become that they cleverly create their own rebels, who are, in fact, never rebellious enough to change the boundaries of the culture that gives them life. The fruits of such 'rebellion' are nothing more than manifestations of the materialistic narcissism that restricts all of us within its narrow borders.

In such a world, *real* rebellion might, strangely enough, be part of the decision to pursue a religious life. While rebellion, perhaps, doesn't explain our loyalty to our churches entirely, it may be an ingredient, and, if it is, it surely comes from a sense of revulsion at a world which encourages us to reject ourselves, encourages us to live lives that are not ours, encourages us to run from the core truth that our existence on this earth is intimately bound up with the mystery of love as a value in our lives.

I once had an experience on a bus in Dublin one rainy evening in the Spring of

1994. The bus was stuck in traffic on O'Connell Bridge and I had a strange feeling that all the trees in front of me on O'Connell Street were growing just for me. I also felt that the countless men and women who paced the wet pavements on their ways home from work were as much a part of me as the breath that filled my lungs. I felt my own life meant nothing in isolation from my fellows. I felt I had no destiny. Only the destiny of my race and planet home had meaning for me. Where had my proud and callous ego gone? Where were the defences I had carefully erected around myself? Why was I falling in love with this feeling that there are no enemies apart from the enemies we choose to create?

That experience was over almost as soon as it had begun, a speck of dust on the path of eternity. The friend I was on my way to visit that night has no memory of me telling her of my experience, even though she is a committed religious person who would naturally take an interest in such things. What was a major event for me did not feature on her radar. It features to this day on mine, not in terms of its force, but in terms of the memory it has left behind. I look back on that experience and believe it to have been an encounter with heaven, an encounter with the selfless, poetic blessing at the heart of human living. Whatever despair I now feel in relation to my life is held in paradoxical balance to that beautiful experience. We are all the Beloveds.

The strength of the other side of the paradox is also, however, very real. In as much as we are blessed, we are also broken. Lurking behind whatever facades we have constructed there is a sense of fracture, a disconnectedness, a discord. I used to be surprised to find that people I thought were perfect were in fact imperfect, but I am not surprised by this any more because I have come to accept that imperfection is part of the human condition. And fundamental to this imperfection is the loneliness of being a human person. When I started talking about loneliness in church circles, I used to apologise for being perhaps too personal, but the more I have spoken about it the more I have come to appreciate it as a universal phenomenon. There is deep existential loneliness in people and we tend to treat it a bit like we treat a drunken guest at a dinner party – we try to pretend it is not there by ignoring it and hoping it will stop. But it doesn't stop and often it drives people into all sorts of crazy behaviour, behaviour which we hope will distract us. Religion can be one of these distractions, particularly when it abdicates its role in helping us to come to terms with the isolation we experience as people and opts instead to temporarily numb the pain. Religion in this sense can be a powerful narcotic. Like opium it can engender feelings of euphoria and ecstasy. It can convince us that it is good for us in a way that discards the sufferings inflicted on those who do not belong to its ranks. Such religions often succeed in putting their adherents into such a spin that 'good' works become a mere distraction from our loneliness and not deep responses to the human condition forged in the suffering heart. The results of this can be catastrophic. Accepting our brokenness, however, is a deeply religious thing to do because only by doing so can we cultivate an ability to give ourselves in acts of love to others.

I want to develop this idea a little further and I want to do so by recalling

Henri Nouwen's treatment of the wounded healer.[36] The term 'wounded healer' will be familiar to many as a concept used by Carl Jung to describe the effective physician as the one who is in touch with their own wounds. So central was this concept to Jung's understanding that it forms the title of one of the seminal biographies on the man.[37] Like Jung, Nouwen saw that by accepting the many ways in which we are fractured ourselves we learn to be more present to the fractures in others. By entering into our own pain and sorrow we actually creates bonds with other people who are also suffering. Care ceases to be an arbitrary interest in helping the less fortunate, which may be given or taken away according to our own personal fancies. Instead care becomes an exchange between equals, forged in the knowledge that we all suffer.

Minister, religious educator and scholar, David Robb, has revisited the story of the *Good Samaritan*, a story which Nouwen suggested we recall *The Parable of the Wounded Healer*. Robb quite rightly attends to an aspect of the story that is frequently overlooked, that is the status of the Samaritan who stops to help the wounded man.[38]

The story is set in the context of a conversation between the Christ and a young lawyer, who is interested in knowing how to acquire eternal life. The lawyer knows the law – he must love God and his neighbour – but he is interested in defining what exactly is meant by the term 'neighbour,' a legitimate question for a lawyer, we might think. The Christ then tells the story of the unfortunate man who was attacked on his way to Jerusalem.

As the story proceeds we hear of certain people passing by the wounded man, people we would today expect to stop. At the time, though, these people would have rendered themselves ritually unclean if they had stopped and helped – maybe we can understand their dilemma somewhat more in this context. Then, along comes the Samaritan. The Samaritan would have been a controversial character to those listening to this story. He was descended from those who had allowed the Jewish faith to be compromised by over familiarity with the Assyrian culture that swamped the northern kingdom of Israel after the Assyrian invasion of the eight century BCE. Unlike the Jews of the southern Kingdom, Judah, who had withstood the oppression of the later Babylonian captivity, the Samaritans had given in, and in so doing they had betrayed the ancient covenant.

For this reason, the Samaritan was not a person the Christ's audience would have easily identified with. We can imagine, perhaps, that those listening to the parable were about to conclude that the wounded man was our neighbour. Maybe they thought they could appreciate the story without even considering the Samaritan. Then, however, the Christ asked the crucial question: who acted as neighbour?

How difficult it must have been for the listeners to answer that question. The rabbi was asking them to commend the actions of a turncoat from the north.

Important to our discussion is what allowed, empowered, facilitated, urged, or compelled the Samaritan to stop. Both Nouwen and Robb invite us to consider the outcast status of the man. He was an alien in a land where he was not welcome. He was a vulnerable man in a hostile world. He was a man who carried his wounds and these wounds invited him to reach out beyond his own pain and attend to the wounds of another person.

Nouwen reminds us in another place that the origins of the word 'care' lie in the gothic word 'kara' which means to lament.[39] There is a special quality to the care given by those people who are in touch with their own laments, their own pain. When people attempt to care without paying heed to this universal aspect of the human condition, the care can easily become patronising and counter productive. When we lose sight of our own pain we assume the status of the helper who has power over the afflicted. I have seen this at play many times in the care we offer to older people in care homes and hospitals. The failure on the part of some staff to live in the knowledge of time's relentless and victorious march over us all results in an unhealthy approach to patient welfare that sees the patient as childlike and immature. I have learnt to respect the sometimes cantankerous approach of the old person to their carers as a demand that the universal nature of suffering be acknowledged in the delivery of care, because when care does not come from our sense of common suffering it is demeaning and sometimes cruel.

Acknowledging the universal nature of suffering does not mean we can only relate to those people who have suffered in a similar fashion to ourselves. It means, rather, that we get in touch with the part of ourselves that is aching. Even those lucky enough to have avoided significant external distress in their lives have aspects to their natures which are difficult to bear. There is hurt and pain in all of us and we can choose to spend our lives trying to avoid it, or we can learn to embrace it as one important part of a multi layered identity. The people who manage to do this are not sombre, depressive killjoys. In my experience they tend to be people who exude humour and light heartedness in their approach to life. The suffering and pain of life does not define their existence. It merely informs their overarching attitudes to others.

Liberal religious communities are often places filled with anxiety about their future. People like Tillich, Nouwen and Robb remind us that corporate self preservation is not a feature of the spiritual life. The beloved community rejects the anxiety engendered by numerical decline, opting instead to accept the spiritual invitation to stand in tender, cosmic solidarity with our fellows, a solidarity forged from a sense of shared suffering with others. If religion is a response to the spiritual, then its business should be a response to this invitation.

There is a responsibility on all of us to create boundaries to preserve our own health, safety and personal space. There is also a responsibility on us to ensure that boundaries do not become defence barriers where we shut ourselves in and others out of our self obsessed cocoons. We must learn to see the wounds of others – and indeed the wounds we carry ourselves – not as problems to be solved, not as emergencies to be rushed at, but as gifts to be held with tenderness and care.

Beloved community simply invites us to live our individuality more profoundly by honestly accepting our wounds and allowing these wounds to forge bonds with other people. We are all broken. But we are all blessed. This is a central paradox in every life. As Mary Oliver put it:

Tell me about despair, yours, and I will tell you mine.
Meanwhile the world goes on.
Meanwhile the sun and the clear pebbles of the rain
are moving across the landscapes,
over the prairies and the deep trees,
the mountains and the rivers.

Meanwhile the wild geese, high in the clean blue air,
are heading home again.
Whoever you are, no matter how lonely,
the world offers itself to your imagination,
calls to you like the wild geese, harsh and exciting—
over and over announcing your place
in the family of things.[40]

Chapter Seven

Nature in the Beloved Community

SO FAR we have explored our skirmishes with Divinity in relation to our own interior lives and in relation to our interactions with other people. However, the earth and the wider cosmos of which it is a tiny part have a claim to Divinity as well. As a living organism the earth is alive with mystery and if any of you have ever climbed a mountain or looked out to sea you'll know that it has its own truth and wisdom also.

One of my favourite people, Nick, is an avowed atheist. One evening as I was about to leave his home after some post pub gin and tonics, I noticed a picture on the wall near the door. My observation was noted and Nick told me that what I was looking at was, in fact, a picture of the Milky Way. We had just spent three or four hours debating the God question, but this picture brought us to silence. For a few moments we stood there, enthralled by the splendour of it all. Our solar system was not even discernible amidst the cloud of light and gas, but wordlessly we both acknowledged in those moments that we were part of this great thing. We were part of it and it was part of us. Atheist and minister of religion stood united before the awe inspiring sight of our galactic home.

Whether we like it or not, our lives are lived in the midst of matter. There has never been an idea, a prayer or an action that was not linked in some profound way with the earth. In this sense we can understand why many primal religious traditions proclaimed the earth to be sacred. In the Celtic tradition, for instance, every river contained a goddess; every mountain was sculpted by some sacred encounter; and every wind was scented with the breath of the Creator. For the Celt the earth was imbued with its own divinity and this divinity was at play long before the salt of the ocean first lodged within the pores of human skin.

Science has helped us to understand the mechanism by which the human being first, victoriously, crawled out of the pond. The work of biologists, chemists and physicists allows us to see the many ways in which our origins and indeed our destiny as human beings is closely linked to the origins and destiny of our planet home and the other life forms that share it.

It is puzzling to think that such information has not led to more widespread appreciation and respect for the natural world. Instead the planet suffers. Intensive farming has turned fertile ground into desert. Factories have filled the air with poisons and even the ocean groans from filth and over fishing – all this at a time when science highlights the many levels on which we are linked to the world around us. It is frightening to consider that the earth will not stall its decline to accommodate the human race. The more we sully her, the sicker she becomes. We need to rediscover our natural relationship with the earth and I want to say that we begin the journey of rediscovering our relationship with her by rediscovering our bodies.

Over the last few years a glut of television programmes have appeared on our screens aimed at sorting out difficult children. Most of them follow a similar format. Stern but effective nanny arrives into a family home. She mildly humiliates the parents for their shortcomings and then sets them straight. I've enjoyed being reminded of just how clever children are in terms of coming up with behaviour, often unpremeditated, to get the attention of their parents.

Some months ago on one such programme a little boy was refusing to eat. His calorie intake was dangerously low and his parents were naturally worried. I felt a particular interest in this case because his extreme behaviour seemed to be craving a level of attention above and beyond the normal childhood games. It turned out his problems with food began when his father moved back into the family home following a short period of separation. What characterised that family reunion was the complete absence of anything close to communication. The parents freely admitted that they thought it best just to ignore the problems that led to the separation and get on with raising their kids. When the child psychologist heard this she invited the parents to see their son's problem with food as his attempt to stop the family moving on. The son was in fact calling out to the parents to resolve their difficulties in a more honest and candid fashion. When the parents did this their son started to eat.

Many therapists will tell you that deep psychological issues often reveal themselves in terms of how we relate to sex and in terms of how we relate to food. The body is in some ways a screen, projecting what's really going on. Both food and sex are experiences which we can share with others. The body's refusal to engage with others on these levels usually points to something of great importance, some great discrepancy that wants to find balance.

Many of us have learnt to see our bodies as machines for carrying our minds around and nothing else, but the behaviour of that little boy invites us to contemplate the body as a thing of far greater significance. In order to get closer to that significance, we need to examine the ways in which we have become alienated from our bodies in the first place.

I suspect that at the heart of the alienation lies the idea that matter is less important than other aspects of our identity. Specifically for thousands of years the body has had to play second fiddle to the soul. Plato thought the soul was like a bird locked in a cage whose only hope of liberation was death. In India many Hindus have explained their comparative understanding of the soul, atman, as being like air trapped in an earthen vessel. In this case the vessel is the body and the task facing all of us is to break the jar so that the individual soul can merge with the world soul – which in the case of Hinduism is called the Brahman.

In more recent centuries the second class status of the body has been compounded by Enlightenment philo sophies based on the idea that we are because we think. Descartes, the father of modern philosophy and the man who coined the phrase, cogito ergo sum – I think therefore I am – saw nature divided into mind and matter. This Cartesian dualism has exacerbated the already harmful Judaeo Christian notion that the body was sinful and in need of a fig leaf before God. It is interesting to consider that in the Garden of Eden the fig leaf came after the commandment to subdue the earth. Perhaps there is a correlation. Perhaps we started to reject our bodies soon after we learnt to dominate the planet.

The result is not just undesirable. It is catastrophic. We are perhaps going to be the first species to accurately predict our own annihilation, not because some vengeful pie in the sky God is angry, but because we are killing the very thing that sustains our lives: the earth. We are killing the earth, because, like our bodies, it is made of matter, and therefore we see it as less worthy than the 'spiritual'. It is worth considering the tragic irony that our materialism is not spiritual enough while our spiritualities do not adequately honour the material.

Christians who are aware of this have tried, through exegetical and hermeneutical endeavours, to redress the balance in favour of a theory that posits the human subject as guardian of the planet. In their thinking God did not ask us to subdue the earth, but, rather, look after it. From where I'm standing this is not enough. If we are to fathom a way of caring for the earth, it must begin with an acknowledgement that the earth does not belong to us, either as our own property or as something given to us to look after on a sub contract from God. It is we, rather, who belong to the earth – an insight of many primal peoples and a sentiment allegedly given poetic expression by the Native American, Chief Seattle.[41] Seattle, like many from the world's primal traditions, knew that there's not a cell in our bodies that did not in some way come from the earth.

It is possible to argue that the myths contained in the biblical account were appropriate to their age. They are certainly not appropriate to ours. The God previous generations relied on to intervene is dead. Our age knows that it is possible for millions of people to die from war and starvation and God does not intervene. Using Ockham's razor, if we really must, the chances are that God will not intervene to set right the environmental problem either. It is up to us to re discover the sacred import of the earth by recognising that before Bibles, Korans or Sutras, the earth was here, expressing its nature in fire, earth, water and wind, gradually moving towards the day when a chemical collision would give birth to our race.

In his poem, *I Sing the Body Electric*, Walt Whitman wrote

Nose, nostrils of the nose, and the partition,
Cheeks, temples, forehead, chin, throat, back of
the neck, neck slue,
Strong shoulders, manly beard, scapula, hind
shoulders, and the ample side round of the chest,
Upper arm, armpit, elbow socket, lower arm, arm
sinews, arm bones,
Wrist and wrist joints, hand, palm, knuckles,
thumb, forefinger, finger joints, finger nails,
Broad breast front, curling hair of the breast,
breast bone, breast side,
Ribs, belly, backbone, joints of the backbone,
Hips, hip sockets, hip strength, inward and
outward round, man balls, man root,
Strong set of thighs, well carrying the trunk above,
Leg fibres, knee, knee pan, upper leg, under leg,
Ankles, instep, foot ball, toes, toe joints, the heel;
All attitudes, all the shapeliness, all the belongings
of my or your body or of any one's body, male or
female....
O I say these are not the parts and poems of the
body only, but of the soul,
O I say now these are the soul![42]

Now that's a rather novel idea for the nineteenth century gentleman to express. In a world in which body and soul were seen as completely separate things, in a world blindly accepting Cartesian dualism,

Whitman invites us to consider the body and soul as one thing – the body electric. When Whitman self published *Leaves of Grass* he was heavily criticised for its emphasis on sexuality and body parts. This would support the claim that not only were the material and non material seen as separate, at least by the chattering class, one was also clearly seen as shameful and of less value.

The more I observe the poetics of my body the more inclined I am to see it as something as close to my soul as the scent of a rose is to the air it fills. And, something I have found helpful in this contemplation is John O'Donohue's idea that our soul does not live in the body. The body, rather, lives in the soul.[43] If the body is in the soul, then it joins the rest of the material world in being shrouded and filled with value, infinitude and mystery. The body electric opens the door which allows us to consider the planet electric. When Julian of Norwich saw the entire created order in her hand, or when Meister Eckhart said that in the innermost part of our selves God creates the universe, they were surely pointing to this way of seeing ourselves and the world in which we live.

Understanding our bodies not as self contained units but as manifestations of the ever expanding cosmos gives us an ability to identify and embrace the universe in ways that transcend Enlightenment dualism.

The body is not something separate from what is most sacred. It is part of the sacred dance that has been going on since time began. For a little boy on television it offered a prophetic protest, calling upon a man and woman to seek greater integrity in their relationship. I wonder if we really listened to our bodies what prophesies might emerge for us?

Walt Whitman, a man who found sincere prayer in his sweaty armpits – what an image – sang of the body electric. He sang because he knew that Descartes had it wrong. He sang because he learned that at a very deep level indeed, the body is joined in origin and destiny to the debris that floats around the very borders of our universe. He sang because he learnt that the body, in as much as it is a doorway into the cosmos, is also the doorway the cosmos uses to get into us. He sang because he re imagined love, not as passive submission to the external, but as a celebration of our connection to the ever expanding eternal. He sang the body electric because the exciting, thrilling and stimulating energy of the Divine is alive in our cells and we share these cells with the entire universe.

In the same way that the body is not a machine that carries the mind, the universe is not merely the ground upon which we stand. It is actually the ground from which we come. We are of it and cannot exist independently from it. From our Sun to Pluto to the most distant star, it, too, is shrouded in a mystery which we are unlikely to explain away before we die out as a species. It has the capacity to silence the discussion between an atheist and a minister and remind both of its infinite value. While it may or may not be God, it is certainly of God; it is part of the deepest mystery we are aware of; it is all we have to look at, and what a sight! The material world is not only the earliest of all revelations, it is the most enduring.

In an age characterised by doubt and uncertainty, the problems facing our planet are, by contrast, certain and concrete. Many argue that human self interest will ultimately redress the balance and save the earth. They place their faith in the human drive to survive and imagine that sufficient steps will be taken to ensure the planet survives in such a way as to sustain human life. I very much doubt human self interest's capacity to do this. Self interest that ignores the interests of the creatures and systems we share the planet with has led to the problems. How can it possibly solve them? The solution will surely have to involve a re imagining of how we fit into the overall scheme of things.

Beloved community, then, is a place that courageously embarks on this project of re imagining. It does so because to be human is to be of the earth; to be human is to belong here as embodied people, linked to the cosmos by our cells; to be human is to search for that place where the planet's connection to us is apparent. While we may not understand the precise nature of the connection, no life can be complete without honouring its mystery. We are bodies electric, part of the body electric, singing to the cosmos electric that gives us a home.

Epilogue

We could not walk, so on our knees we
crawled
The downward spiral path we prayed
would take us to
Some unknown holy totem pole of peace.

Nor silence could we keep, so arrows sent
The words that pierce the muffled silent
groaning womb
That never fully wants to give us birth.

We could not hope, but hopes we ever
sung
Despite the fact they sadly clung to
yesterday,
And had no place with wounds our lives
inflict.

No eternal rest or bliss I seek!
Just hang me, Life, on holy totem poles of
peace,
So others on the outmost circling rung,

Might know another crawled this way in
song.

Notes

[1] Michel Foucault, a leading light for many a postmodernist, refused to be categorised as one throughout his life.

[2] For a fuller account of Kurt Cobain's life and death, readers may be interested in Charles R Cross, <u>Heavier Than Heaven – A Biography of Kurt Cobain</u>. Hyperion Books, 2001.

[3] Six Feet Under, Season Five, Episode Ten. Written by Kate Robin. Directed by Adam Davidson.

[4] The copyright on Kurt Cobain's suicide is not clear to this author. It can be viewed at http://www.hotshotdigital.com/WellAlwaysRemember.2/KurtCobainNote.html.

[5] Bentham, Jeremy, <u>The Panopticon</u>. 1791. This document is available for download from: http://cartome.org/panopticon2.htm. Bentham's ideas were first raised in a series of letters in 1787.

[6] Foucault, Michel. <u>Discipline and Punish: The Birth of The Prison</u>. Translated from the original French by Alan Sheridan. Gallimard, 1977.

[7] See <u>Michel Foucault: Beyond Structuralism and Hermeneutics</u>. Second Edition. Hubert L. Dreyfus and Paul Rabinow (eds). University of Chicago Press, 1982.

[8] See Sarup, Madan, <u>An Introductory Guide to Post Structuralism and Postmodernism</u>.

University of Georgia Press, 1993. "Lyotard and Postmodernism," will be of particular value.

[9] I came across this insight from O'Casey in the programme which accompanied the Glasgow Citizen's Theatre production of In The Shadow of a Gunman, 2006.

[10] Sarfraz Manoor, Instant Karma for the Rich and Famous, The Guardian, Tuesday, June 15th 2004.

[11] Heelas, Paul & Woodhead, Linda (with Benjamin Seel, Bronislaw Szerszynski and Karin Tusting), The Spiritual Revolution: Why Religion is Giving Way to Spirituality, Blackwell, 2005.

[12] James Joyce. Letter, 22 Nov. 1902, in which Joyce announced his intention to leave Ireland permanently. From a private collection. Quoted from The Columbia Dictionary of Quotations.

[13] Nietzsche, Friedrich. Thus Spoke Zarathustra: A Book for All and None. Translated and prefaced by Walter Kaufmann, The Modern Library, 1995.

[14] Royce, Josiah, The Philosophy of Loyalty. Vanderbilt University Press, 1995. Page 47

[15] Royce, Josiah, The Problem of Christianity, Catholic University of America Press, 2001. Page 357

[16] See Dunayevskaya, Raya, <u>Marxism and Freedom, from 1776 until Today.</u> Humanity Books, 2000. Also <u>Philosophy and Revolution: from Hegel to Sartre and from Marx to Mao</u>. Columbia University Press, 1989.

[17] Beiser, Frederick (ed), <u>The Cambridge Companion to Hegel</u>. Cambridge University Press, 1993

[18] Wolin, Richard, <u>The Seduction of Unreason</u>. Princeton University Press, 2006

[19] Bailey, Derrick Sherwin, <u>Homosexuality and the Western Christian Tradition</u>. Archon Books, 1975.

[20] Ibid.

[21] See McNeill, John J., <u>The Church and the Homosexual</u>. Beacon Press, 1993

[22] Beach, George Kimmich, <u>Questions for the Religious Journey: Finding Your Own Path</u>. Skinner House Books, 2002. Previously published under the title, <u>If Yes is the Answer, What is the Question</u>, and cited here from a sermon delivered by Rev Dr John A. Buehrens, 'On Being Otherwise,' delivered at First Parish in Bedford, 14th November 1999.

[23] Martineau, James, <u>The Seat of Authority in Religion</u>. Longmans, Green & Co., 1890

[24] George Chryssides from the University of Wolverhampton has written a concise and revealing online account of Martineau's

position.   The article can be viewed at:
http://web.uni
marburg.de/religionswissenschaft/journal/dis
kus/chryssides_2.html

[25] This story was often cited by the Dutch theologian, Fr Henri Nouwen, to illustrate how we minister to each other by being honest about our own shortcomings.

[26] O'Donohue, John, Anam Cara, HarperCollins, 1997

[27] Walter Kaiser wrote an excellent historical survey of the fool for The Dictionary of the History of Ideas. Charles Scribner's Sons, 1973. Unfortunately this title has been out of print for many years. However, a collaboration between the University of Virginia and the Board of the *Journal of the History of Ideas*, with Charles Scribner's Sons permission, has made many of the original articles available online. They can be viewed at:
http://etext.virginia.edu/DicHist/dict.html.
A revised version of the original dictionary was published in 2006 and edited by Maryanne Cline Howowitz. It is available in six print volumes and also as an ebook from Charles Scribner's Sons.

[28] www.boulderbellygrams.com contains a large selection of Nasruddin stories.

[29] James 5:16, 'Confess your faults one to another, and pray one for another, that ye may be healed.' (King James Version)

[30] Gay, Peter (ed), The Freud Reader. Vintage, 1995.

[31] Ibid. Page 24

[32] Tillich, Paul, Shaking the Foundations, Charles Scribner's Sons, New York, in 1955. This material was downloaded from Religion Online

[33] Ibid.

[34] The American writer, Thomas Moore, offers a beautiful and insightful depiction of how our imperfections can be re imagined. See: Moore, Thomas, Care of the Soul – How To Add Depth and Meaning to your Everyday Life. Piatkus, 1992. Also: Moore, Thomas, Soul Mates – Honouring the Mysteries of Love and Relationships. Element Books, 1994

[35] Nouwen, Henri, Life of the Beloved. The Crossroad Publishing Co. 1992. Pages 25 26.

[36] See Nouwen, Henri, The Wounded Healer. Doubleday Publishing, 1972

[37] Dunne, Claire, Carl Jung: Wounded Healer of the Soul. Continuum International Publishing Group, 2002.

[38] Robb, David, 'The Wounded Healer.' A sermon delivered at All Souls Church (Unitarian Universalist), New York, September

1st, 2002. Available from the church website: www.allsoulsnyc.org

[39] Nouwen, Henri, <u>Out of Solitude: Three Meditations for the Christian Life</u> (Second revised edition). Ave Maria Press, 2004.

[40] Oliver, Mary, <u>New and Selected Poems</u>. Beacon Press, 1992. Page 110

[41] Controversy surrounds the origins of the words attributed to Seattle. They most likely originated in a film script, penned by Tim Perry, for a film called 'Home'. Whoever uttered these words, the fact remains they are inspiring and worthy of our consideration, irrespective of source.

[42] Whitman, Walt, <u>Leaves of Grass</u>. Airmont Publishing Company, 1965. Pages 82 88.

[43] O'Donohue, John, <u>Anam Cara</u>. HarperCollins, 1997.

Printed in the United Kingdom
by Lightning Source UK Ltd.
119895UK00001B/205-258